A
butterfly
in the
Garden

A true story
beginning with haiku

*A caterpillar
knows little of wings before;
its time has arrived.*

© Annie

A butterfly in the Garden
By Annie

Published by:
Godsign Institute
337 Ripple Road
Indianapolis, IN 46208
www.godsigninstitute.com
866-450-8449
317-410-5224

In association with
Taped Editions, Inc.
5160 East 65th Street
Indianapolis, IN 46220
www.tapededitions.com
800-850-1701
317-849-1700

Library of Congress Cataloging-in-Publication Data
Annie Truesdell
A butterfly in the Garden/Annie
ISBN 9781887356107
1. God – Miscellanea   2. Spirituality – Miscellanea
3. Death – Miscellanea   4. Communication with Spirit
5. Poetry – Miscellanea   6. Title

TXU10018900164.   TXu1-189-164

Printed in USA

First Edition Paperback 2010

Dedicated to You

You love someone very much
but you may not think they can
communicate with you anymore.

Your loved one knows differently
and wishes to say Hi to you,
for they know they can
and they know you will hear them.

It is why you are holding this book in the First Place.

Chapter I
A Caterpillar Travels from Seen to Unseen...

It began the day Gary died.

I didn't know anything had begun, but begun it had.

To me this was nothing but a terrible ending and I was stopped, dead in my tracks. I should say forgive the bad pun, but please don't. I experienced the essence of that phrase the moment I heard. I felt dead in my tracks and didn't move, not for a long time...until the shaking started.

It was early November of '99. The phone rang and I was getting dinner ready as one of my sons answered. "Mom...for you." I knew right away it was my friend Paul, I know his voice so well; the way he says, "Hey, babe." He choked it out: Gary had died a few hours before. Gary's wife Joy had left for work early in the morning and it hadn't been time for Gary to get up. She kissed him, said goodbye, and left. That night she came home. Gary had never gotten up out of bed; he was gone. Paul continued, "Annie, they think his heart ruptured...Sweetie, are you there?" I couldn't catch my breath and I couldn't speak without it. "Ann. Please say something."

I was able to get out a whispered, "Yes, I'm here."

Paul went on, "Marianne and I are on our way over to Joy's right now. Are you going to be okay? We will call you later tonight, I promise." He was having a hard time keeping control; you could hear it in his voice and having to be the one to tell me...it is one of the hardest things you ever do for someone you love. He said goodbye and still I just stood there.

My son was staring at me with a large questioning look. "It's going to be okay, honey," I said. "I just found out Gary has died and it is going to make me very sad for awhile, but it is going to be okay." He told me he was very sorry and left the room. He was just a little guy at the time and it is hard to

4

watch someone you love in pain over a death, regardless of age.

Oh, my God, Gary...you're gone. It was then the shaking started.

I moved myself out of the house and onto the back deck. I had to be alone for as long as I could get away with it. My husband Martin wasn't yet home from work and dinner needed to be finished. It was then I realized I was going to be spending the next innumerable days, weeks, months doing nothing but crying. Homework needed to get done, food cooked, cleaned up, life's chores taken care of...nothing but crying....

His laughter is gone. I just sat there sobbing as quietly as a mouse wracked with grief. I realize that is a weird thought, but have you ever heard one? You know what I mean if you have ever found yourself crying as hard as you can cry, trying not to make a sound while doing it.

I had lost family before and that had hurt terribly. My grandfather had died just a few months before, but somehow this was different. This was the death I was unprepared to deal with. There are people in your life you just always believe you will see again: sons, daughters, brothers, sisters, parents, friends. This is the pain that leaves you breathless when you realize that belief is a luxury, not a right. A hard Truth in life...still I shook.

Just the smallest sliver of a silver moon hung clipped in the sky. I wonder if you ever forget the moments right after you hear someone you dearly love has died.

Gary was my brother, one that I was very close to and deeply loved. I should say for the purists out there, he was not my brother by blood. Gary was a brother I chose: one I added to my family as a young woman and one I adored. We had started out as friends and become family. I had last seen him a few months before, on a perfect night in May when he and Joy had come to my 40th birthday party. I had spoken to him on the phone in October, just a couple weeks before, and now I would never do that again. I had met Gary when I was 20 and now I was 40. We had been so close for such a long time; not enough time, and yet now it was a lifetime.

It was the end of 1999. I had been as excited as most, and looking forward to the holidays and the start of a new millennium. To be able to say you were alive at the beginning of the year 2000 was quite a thing to be able to say. Now I realize that depends on whose calendar you go by, but mine read that we were coming to the end of one millennium and the beginning of the next. It was a big deal. Something you tell your grandchildren, great-grandchildren. The excitement was palpable. So much of the world was getting ready for it, coming together for a special moment in history. That was the good news. The bad news: our computers were quitting at midnight, walking off the job, as it were. So many of the world's computers might not be able to handle this particular tick of the clock; or so the theory went. Remember those months?

Well, I didn't care about any of it anymore. The holidays didn't matter; the turning of anything didn't really matter to me. The month of November came and went and I cried my way through it. I took care of my children and my husband and my job; but in, through, and around this time mostly I cried. I also found myself working through the grief in another way, besides all the tears, and my mind knew it was an unreasonable way, a way that would seem "crazy" to many, if not most. But at this point in our dialogue, you can answer this question: Did I care?

I tried to work my way through the grief and pain by continuing a "conversation" with Gary "in my head." There was too much left unsaid between us; too many conversations still in front of us. Too many things had happened that I needed to talk to him about. Of course, I knew the dialogue was one-sided...me telling him how very sad I was for him, how much I hurt for Joy, how sorry I felt for me. How much I was going to miss him, his friendship, his hugs…his laughter. I knew I was just talking to myself. Yeah, well, did I care? What I didn't expect and truly couldn't have prepared for was when Gary showed back up, in real time and in my real life. And God knows, it was in a way that only someone who was a master showman like Gary could have pulled off….

***

The first day I didn't cry within the first few hours of waking was a little over a month after Gary died. It was the day my brother John, this one by blood, and his wife Jacquelyn were having an annual Christmas gathering of friends. John and Jacquelyn are a very warm, generous, and loving couple. I adore them both. I have shared a group of friends with them for a very long time and once a year, around Christmas, this particular group gets together. It is a group of friends that have known and loved each other for many, many years. We had gotten to that stage in our lives where children seemed to be everywhere and jobs and other commitments were in charge, we weren't. This night might very well be the only night that year we would all see each other. There are no children attending this party, no new friends, no one's parents; it's just us. This is one party we all try our best to make.

The kinship of this group is very special in many ways, one being that the love felt and shown for one another is the unconditional love of a true friendship grown over many years. All of us can be ourselves at this party, completely and without reservation. You may show your ass at this party, proverbial or otherwise, and you *know* you will get talked about and that's perfectly okay with you. Each of us has had at least one turn at sipping too much of whatever punch we had concocted for ourselves. Everybody's had a year where it all seemed to be too much and needed one night to totally blow off whatever steam had built up, and to know they were safe while doing it. Everyone's had a turn at playing the party's fool and we all know that we are going to be just as loved and just as accepted the day after the party as we were the day before; perhaps more so. It's a very special band of friends, indeed.

It was now the one evening, the one holiday event that year I was excited about. I had just lost a very dear friend and Martin and I were going to spend the evening with other friends we deeply loved and rarely got to see anymore. Being with these people was even more special now than it had ever been. I needed this party, badly, and I wasn't going to let anything get me down—at least not that day. I was finally feeling happy about something and I was excited as we pulled into my brother's driveway. Martin gets out of the car and looks up into the clear night sky and sees a shooting star. I told him, "Hold on, dear, it could be a crazy night." I told myself to do the same…just hold on.

John and Jacquelyn are exquisite hosts. They have a lovely home and a wonderful way of making sure you realize when you cross their threshold you are in your home away from home. Everybody was gathered in the downstairs family room. For that night it is the party room. It contains the bar, pool table area, large television for whatever game is on, a blazing fireplace, and of course, the doors that look out onto the back garden. It is perfect for a party.

We had all been there long enough to hug each other and have a cocktail. I was standing by myself for a moment, leaning against the far wall, taking in the view. I honestly wanted to absorb the room. All these friends, all these smiles, all this love gathered in one spot. I wanted to somehow fill myself up with all the feelings, experiences, and emotional comfort I could get my greedy hands on. While I was doing this, out of the corner of my mind a thought appeared…"Oh, babe! What a great party! Can I come?"

Gary? Oh no, Annie, no you don't! I got angry, very angry with myself. You are not going to get yourself started thinking you are "talking" to Gary right now. He is gone and you have got to stop these ridiculous conversations…thinking he can somehow "hear" you! Enough! Just get a hold of yourself, please, and stop it.

And then I threw what I knew to be impossibility out to the "thoughts" in my head: "Gary, if you are really there, I will win the pool tournament tonight, you will attend a great party, and we can talk about it in the morning." I stood up away from the wall and headed out into the room.

Now of course, I win the pool tournament, or there would be no tale to tell. But as with most "games" in life, it wasn't that I won that is so memorable, so incredible. It was the *way* it was won.

***

That I would have anything to do with winning the pool tournament that year was not possible to me. There was no way it would occur. I believed that because the very last thing I wanted to do that night was play pool. I had a room full of people I wanted to spend time with, listen to, and enjoy. I had no intention of wasting time getting little colored balls into tiny pockets. I was in no mood to spend a moment of this particular night trying to remember whether I was striped or solid. However, just begging out was not really an option. If a woman doesn't play, one of the guys can't either; everyone plays so everyone can play. I suppose I could have raised a ruckus and just refused that year but I was there to have fun, not cause myself more grief.

The tournament is played as the party rolls along. At the beginning of the evening, each woman pulls a guy's name out of the hat. She is then the pool partner with that particular gentleman until they lose. The game played: your standard eight ball. The only house rule: you may not play with your spouse. Did I mention this group is also rather intelligent?

That year I pulled Ross's name out of the hat. I love Ross. He is one of the world's best huggers. He is a sports coach and administrator at a public school and one very terrific guy. I felt kind of bad for him because this tournament is a big deal to the guys, bragging rights for the year, as it were. I knew I was going to be playing lousy pool and didn't care. I wanted to get out of playing as fast as I could. Sorry, Ross, I said to myself, there is always next year. And as life would have it, he and I were up first against the pair I would call the number one seeded couple. One of the women at this party, Audrey, can shoot awesome pool. If she draws the name of one of the guys that can shoot great pool, there is your number one seeded team. And that night she did: she drew one of the best pool players of the group, Tino. Good deal, I thought to myself. The sooner this is over, the better! And, as I thought might be the case, Tino and Audrey came close to running the table. Tino was getting ready to shoot the eight ball into the corner, and Ross and I still had most of our balls up on the table. Just as Tino calls the pocket and takes his shot, a "thought" floats into my head.

"Annie, this is important, just for tonight...try to believe, just believe."

Gary?

No, I thought, not Gary; Gary is gone. Please stop doing this to yourself, Ann. This "dialogue" is going on in my head as Tino perfectly shoots the eight ball in the pocket. Then we watch as the cue ball, ever so slowly, heads in the direction of the opposite corner. Well, surely it is going to stop right there. Okay, well, it is going to stop now. It was like watching slow motion video...and it got to a point where we all knew what was going to happen, but there was nothing we could do to stop it. The ball went so slow, but on it went. When the cue ball went into the opposite corner pocket...the chill you get from the tip of your toes all the way to the ends of your hair, all in the same instant...that tingling zipped through me and then the "thought" came into my head..."My dear friend, this is one great party and you know how I love a party! Do you know that there isn't a bad soul here? Try, just for tonight...Believe!" And off the thought went.

Off Gary went? Annie, I don't think so! Please try to get a hold of yourself. What was that? What just happened? Thoughts swirled in my head. Tino and Audrey were, needless to say, bummed. Very gracious and wonderfully good sports about it all, but really bummed. Who wouldn't be?

Ross. Ross was thrilled. He didn't brag or get snotty. I mean, let's face it: we still had most of our balls still on top of the table. But we had just moved on to the next round.

"What was that? What just happened?" I kept asking myself that...just a fluke, just a coincidence. Just a weird moment, and they certainly happen at this party. Ah, but the night was young.

Our next game ended as we were in the middle of playing it. While one of our opponents was shooting a ball into a pocket, another ball kicked off, hit the eight ball, and you know the rest. In a pocket the eight ball went. Game, set, match—Ross and I move on again. I started to get very quiet.

During another game, Ross was across the table from me discussing what shot he should take with one of the guys. He and Audrey's husband were talking strategy and I found myself standing alone just watching the two of them. Another "thought" comes floating into my head: "Annie, honey...believe, just believe." In the same moment, Ross decides what he is going to do and he lets out this coach's yell..."Believe! Just believe!" he shouts. I know my mouth dropped open...I had stereo going.

There were four games Ross and I played that night. We won every game we played. However, not one of those games—not one—did we win because we were the first to get all our balls off the table and sink the eight ball. The eight ball was in charge that night, make no mistake about that, but Ross and I never touched it. Everything that could go wrong with an eight ball went wrong—with our opponents. By the end of the night, Ross and I were that year's champs.

Now, it didn't look like it to anyone in the room, but I was no longer completely "there" anymore. Dazed is a good word here. Amazed would be another word to describe how I felt; and I didn't know what I was supposed to do about what had just happened. Ross looked at me when it was all over, shrugged his shoulders, and let out this ever so male YEEEAAAHHH! I couldn't bring myself to tell anyone. I didn't think piping up with "Uhhh, folks, I'm not really sure Ross and I won because, well, because—something else, someone else did." That just wasn't something I could believe, much less say out loud. Not even this group was ready for a statement like that from me or anybody else. What I did do was drink. I told myself it was all one grand fluke; or somehow maybe, just maybe, it was Gary's way of saying goodbye. I had another cocktail.

Martin and I fell into a bed at John's that night and I just said thank you to the ceiling. Whatever that was, however you did that...you stopped to say goodbye...thanks, Gary...I love you, too!!! It was in time for Christmas...and the tears streamed.

***

I would have thought that was enough, but I had forgotten all about the last part of my challenge to the "thoughts" in my head. I remembered the part about "Gary, if you're really there, I will win the pool tournament." I recalled thinking "…and you'll attend a great party." Those thoughts I remembered. What I had forgotten was the rest of what I had thought in my mind: "…and we'll talk about it in the morning."

The first thought in my head the next morning when I woke was not mine. There is no other way to say that. The first thought that came into my head was definitely NOT one I would have come up with on my own. I wasn't the type; not for a very long time had I been anywhere near the type, especially the night after a party, and certainly not with the deserved hangover I was suffering from. The first "thought" in my head as I woke was, "Annie, while growing up, you recited a prayer at least once a week that you believed in one God, the Father Almighty, Creator of Heaven and earth, of all things Seen and Unseen…. It is now time for you to learn about the *Unseen* part of that statement."

Longing

The hope dreamt which waking forsakes.
Yearning's pain from heart felt aches.
A trick perversely twisted with the treat.
The sentiment that so defines bittersweet.

To endure impatience in life spent
prevented from knowing the scent,
the feeling, or sight of senses sated;
of cravings palled by a spirit elated.

Being pulled by desire's attraction,
yet ties bind preventing reaction
to the taste of joy's sweet lust
before time scatters one's dust.

ahhh…..

To sit within a wish's company,
freely serving oneself to its honey,
euphoric in a moment's belonging.
Rain to the thirst of parched longing.

Intensity flows
inward from the edge of thought.
Reaction cued.

Chapter II
The Signal's Wired In

Winning at pool and all the events that went with that evening and into the next morning were very much like an alarm clock going off in my universe, and I did what any self-respecting caterpillar would do: I hit the snooze button.

I was certainly not about to think that I could have a continuing "dialogue" with someone who was dead. That was not possible to me. The experiences I had the night of the party and into the next morning were incredible. And I mean incredible on every level. They were awesome, breath taking, exciting, scary, and incredible—non-credible—not believable. I told no one about it: not my husband, not any of my friends, no one, because it was so unbelievable to me and I feared would be even more so to them.

But things were going to get even more incredible. Gary was not saying good-bye, he was saying Hello, with and in the Unseen, and he was just getting started. Little did I know that I was going to find myself next in what I can only describe as the "Twilight Zone"...in real life, in real time...again. Scrooge has got nothing on me.

***

Over the next several months I was introduced to and met some wonderfully unique and interesting people. I was continuously surprised because I had little if nothing to do with arranging these meetings. The coincidences kept mounting. I would be introduced to the friend of a friend at a party who received "messages" from the dead. A cousin invites me to a get-together she is having with a medium that will look into our future and speak to the spirits around us. A wonderful woman named Susan starts to work for the same company my husband does, and I come to find out she is studying to be a Spiritualist minister. She had been studying for years and had become quite adept at speaking with and receiving messages from those in the "spirit realm." She is a warm, intelligent, and caring woman who opened my mind to new possibilities.

Even though I never said anything about pool games to these people, they all helped me tremendously in realizing I wasn't totally crazy in believing Gary had "contacted" me. When I look back on it now, I realize I was just being prepared. There have always been plenty of people in society who have "spoken" to the "dead." For the next several months I started to become aware of just how many people there were around me that knew there was an existence after this one and felt comfortable connecting with "It." But that just wasn't me. Okay, so maybe it was not so crazy to think Gary "helped" me with the pool tournament, but I still wasn't about to tell anyone. I had never given that much credence to crystal balls. Magic was something that was best left as entertainment to magicians, a good safe bet. It is a sleight of hand and you must at least have hands, real and solid; however, magic happens with or without a magician "standing" by.

Eleven months had passed since Gary had died. It was Saturday, October 14, 2000, to be exact, and a glorious fall day. I was traveling to my grandmother's home in northern Indiana to help her move some plants. She was moving to Kentucky where my parents lived. My grandfather, whom we lovingly called Pop, had died in July, four months before Gary, and now my Grandmother was moving south. Everything had been arranged for her except for her

16

houseplants; she didn't want the movers in charge of them and she asked if I could help her out.

Both of my grandmothers were gardeners while I was growing up. This grandma was especially good at it. She is a charming Irish woman born and raised in Limerick, Ireland and she always had a type of pixieland garden. I would sit and try to see leprechauns hiding in it when I was a little girl. I am now a gardener myself, and Grandma asked if I would come to get her indoor plants and take them down to her new home. I was honored to be able to help. Besides, it got me out of the house and away from motherhood and all the joys associated with it for a day. I had reached that time as a mom when that was just fine with me.

I headed out early on a wondrous Indian summer morning. The sky was as blue as the sky gets in Indiana. I planned to take my time and stop at some of my favorite antique shops along the way. I have never minded driving alone; it gives me time for me and I find it very relaxing.

I was thinking about all kinds of things driving along that morning. A girlfriend of mine, Cherrie, had been sick. I wondered how she was feeling. What is the best way for me to help the boys get their school projects done and out of the way? I am going to need to make a trip to the arts and crafts store tomorrow. Halloween was coming up, fast. What are they going to dress in this year? I was in the middle of typical mom-on-the-road thoughts. And then he started. "Hi, babe. I'm along for the ride. We're on a rrrooooad trip together."

Gary? No, Ann, no you don't.

A song starts on the radio.

"Baaaabbby, let's cruise away from here…Don't be confused, the way is clear…And if you want it you got it forever…Let the music take your mind….Just release and you will find…You're gonna fly away, glad you're going my way… I love it when we're cruising together…."[1]

It was an old Smokey Robinson and the Miracles tune called "Cruisin'"[2]...and to myself I thought, Yeah, right, Ann. I don't think so! Earth to Annie, Earth to Annie. Keep your eyes on the road and your head down on this planet. Since the pool games, I had been very good at controlling how "loosely" I let my thoughts wander. At the time, I did finally believe that Gary had said good-bye and it was a fantastic gift, but I also believed it was a one-time-only gift. For me to even think I could continue a "conversation" with him after those games was a very scary and therefore dangerous proposition to me. I am an intelligent, rational adult who is trying to keep my marriage happy and raise intelligent, well-adjusted, and loving kids. That, in and of itself, can take a toll on your sanity. I wasn't about to jeopardize my mental health by playing games with and inside my own head. I couldn't imagine trying to contact Gary or anyone else on any kind of regular basis who was dead. I drove on down the road and wondered how Cherrie was feeling.

Half an hour later I am a few hundred miles away in my thoughts. I was thinking about my sister, Rachel, and her husband, Brad. Brad's dad had been ill; his mom had recently died; and I was thinking how much I admired the two of them for all the love, strength, and warmth they gave and shared with those they loved. I worried about the frustrating time ahead for them. I love Rachel very much but I was worried about how much she was working. They were raising two kids, two jobs....

The next "thought" in my head is, "Hey, Annie, beautiful day, huh? What a lovely day for a drive. I have a gift...The next three songs are for you."

What? Gary? Oh, Ann don't even go there with yourself. Just then on the radio the DJ pipes up, "And now for the start of our next ten song set..." and over the radio it comes,

"I would give up forever to touch you, 'cause I know that you feel me somehow...."[3]

Oh my God....

"...When everything feels like the movies, you bleed just to know you're alive...I just want you to know who I am...I just want you to know who I am...I just want you to know who I am...."

It was the first time I had heard this song. The words went through me like an electrical current. It is a powerful song.

It was weeks later before I heard this song again, and months later before I knew who sang it or what album title it was on. It was made popular by *The City of Angels* movie starring Nicholas Cage and Meg Ryan. *The City of Angels* soundtrack[4] had become popular because there was wonderful music from some great artists contained on it. This particular song is called "Iris" and is masterfully performed by a group called the Goo Goo Dolls. They have some tremendous music. However, at the time, all I knew is that I had just been blown away by a song.

The next song starts right in; feel free to sing along—you know this tune.

"It's a little bit funny, this feeling inside. I'm not one of those who can easily hide. I don't have much money, but if I did, I'd buy a big house where we both could live....I know it's not much, but it's the best I can do. My gift is my song, and this one's for you...."[5]

It was Elton John, and doesn't everyone know he is now deservedly titled Sir John, and the song is simply called "Your Song"? *"Your Song"* was the first major hit song for the magnificent songwriting pair of Elton John and Bernie Taupin. (Why Bernie Taupin has not been knighted and also titled Sir Taupin is beyond me.) You will notice the words the next time you hear that song played. Listen to it all the way through and tell me what you would think if it had been you.

19

"...And you can tell everybody this is your song...."
I had to think to breathe.

Next, well, next came music from a group that had meant so much to me, so long ago, for so many reasons...my college days, life at University of Kentucky...around the time in my life that I first met Gary. This is a song that most people my age recognize within the first three notes. It is by Fleetwood Mac and entitled "You Make Loving Fun."

"Sweeeeet wonderful you, you make me happy with the things you do...Oooohh, can it be so? This feeling follows me wherever I go. I never did believe in miracles, but I've a feeling it's time to try. I never did believe in the ways of magic, but I'm beginning to wonder why...."[6]

And I had to get off the road.

***

At the time, I thought it was just perfect timing that the sign for my favorite antique shop was right there. I pulled in and took a deep breath. I told myself, It could have been any of a hundred, no, any of a thousand songs that could have been played on that radio in any order and I would have been able to make something out of it. The idea that Gary somehow... well, you're not even going to go there, Ann. That's insane, absolutely crazy! No, it's more than that and you have to get a grip...it's IMPOSSIBLE for that to have come from Gary. No way. Get out of the car and go look for the side table you were hoping might be inside. And into the world of antiques I went to gather my mind back together.

A little while later I came out with nothing but my head screwed on straight. I knew that the songs that had played over the radio were chosen by a DJ, or these days, the station manager. Period. To think otherwise was ludicrous. My vivid imagination was working on overdrive for a few moments, but that was over. I got back into the car and headed north.

There were commercials playing and before they were over, static showed up. Good, I thought. I hit the seek button a few times and a Beatles tune came on. That was good enough for me. An hour later I was just fine and the weirdness was behind me. In front of me was Grandma's apartment building, and soon after we were visiting.

We talked for a time in her living room and then I took her to lunch at a favorite restaurant. We visited Pop's grave on Notre Dame's campus. This was the one spot that was going to be hardest for her to leave. By now I did realize that if anything of Pop was left, he certainly wasn't here...was he? Thoughts were swirling. It was such a beautiful day, a perfect day for Grandma to get outside. We stayed and tended to some of the flowers around the gravesite. Being fall, it was time to put flowerbeds to bed. After awhile, Grandma and I drove back to her place and I started packing up infinite shades of green houseplants into the June Cleaver mobile, my van.

As I was getting ready to leave, Grandma said there was one more thing she wanted me to take. She led me to a closet and asked me to get a package that was wrapped in brown paper down from the shelf. It was something she wanted me to have. It was rather large and heavy, and she said I should open the wrapping and take a look.

My grandmother had moved to this country with my grandfather when she had been in her forties. All three of her daughters as young women had moved to America a couple years before her in the early '50's. She and Pop came over with their younger sons in 1955.

I had thought about all of this the day before I had made the trip. I was now the age she was when she said good-bye to her family and traveled to America. Would I do that now, at this stage in my life? Could I say good-bye to all my friends and the way of life I had become accustomed to and move to another country? I doubted it; as a matter of fact, I knew not. When I actually stopped to think about it, the faith it took in her husband and in herself to make that leap astounded me.

I try to gently open the paper around this bundle as she is telling me that this had been the one thing she personally carried on the boat trip over to the States. Her grandmother had given it to her. Believe it or not, but I didn't know until that moment that her grandmother's name was Annie. Annie had kept it in her gardens until she had given it to my grandmother.

I unwrapped a beautifully painted statue of the Madonna standing on top of the world with the serpent beneath her feet. She was cloaked in blue and white robes, her hands spread in blessing. I just sat there.

Finally, I looked at my grandma and said that I really couldn't take this from her. "Grandma, she is yours and you need to take this with you to your next home. This statue needs to stay with you!" But my grandmother wouldn't hear of it. She said it was time for her to pass the Madonna on to another granddaughter.

There was no refusal to that.

I wrapped the statue back up and finished packing the van. My grandmother and I hugged, kissed, and then it was time for me to say good-bye. Grandma asked me to be very careful on the trip home. She said she worried about me traveling alone. I smiled and said, "But Grandma, you don't have to worry about me on this trip. I now have extra protection on board, don't you think? That statue is a very special treasure and both of us will make it home safe." She smiled so big.

The day was starting to wind down and I was on my way home. I had about a two and a half hour drive ahead of me and I wanted to get most of the way back before it got too late. I thought I had timed it perfectly. I headed down the road and directed my thoughts back to my list of things that came next. Within the hour I was a million miles away from South Bend in my head and back to the mom-on-the-road thoughts. The boys' school projects...you get warned a lot about the work involved with raising kids: the diapers, laundry, little sleep, but no one warns you about the homework. I was in the middle of thinking about the list of things I was going to need to get for the boys so they could finish their posters, charts, etc. I wonder if I have paper for that one project down in the basement?

"Hey, babe...that was a very precious day, don't you think?" This is the thought that comes into my head, and since it was just as easily my own, I didn't argue and went on with the thought.

Yes, I said to myself, it was very precious, indeed.

"Annie, the next song on the radio is for you."

Before I could react and turn the radio off, the first notes had played and the words sung. It was Elton ...again....

"There's a calm surrender to the rush of day, when the heat of rolling wind can't be turned away. An enchanted moment and it sees me through... Can you feel the love tonight? It is where we are... It's enough for this wide-eyed wanderer that we got this far...It's enough to make kings and vagabonds believe the very best...There's a time for everyone, if they'd only learn that the twisting kaleidoscope moves us all in turn ... " [7]

I shut the radio off.

The next "thought" that enters my head threw me. "Fine, that's fine if you don't want to listen to music right now. I knew that song was a bit much for you at the moment. Switch to AM stations and hit the seek button three times. UK is playing and we can listen to the game."

I was maybe an hour out of South Bend. I was leaving the heart of Notre Dame territory, closing in on Purdue's, and I had never left Indiana University range. It would have never entered my thoughts to try to find a University of Kentucky football game on the radio for a very simple reason: I wouldn't have even thought it possible in this neck of the woods. Nor, to be honest with you, at that moment would I have been interested in listening to any football game on the radio.

But Gary would. You cut Gary and he bled UK blue, as the saying went down south.

My hand was shaking as I turned the radio back on, switched from FM to AM, and hit the seek button three times.

UK was playing LSU...at LSU.

I lost it. I started crying like I hadn't cried since he had died and I started to pull off the road. "No, babe, not here. Don't pull off the road here. There is a perfect place just a mile down. You can make it, remember, you have added 'protection' on board today." I had to smile through the tears.

A mile down the road, on my side of the highway was the *Paradise* Truck Stop. Well, of course it is, I said to myself. I pulled up into a spot and just sat there for a minute trying to stop all the tears. I wasn't sure what to think of what had just happened. It was...I didn't even have words. I got out of the car to get a Coke and stretch my legs, as well as my head.

As I got out and closed the door, I hear, "You've just locked your keys in the car and it is okay," and my car goes "click, click."

Oh, damn, I just locked my keys in the car and it is DEFINITELY NOT OKAY!

I looked in and there were my keys, lying on top of my purse on the passenger seat. I didn't remember setting them there, but there they were. I thought I had closed the moon roof of the van and there was no way in. I looked up and it was open! Yessssssssssss!!! This will be okay....

It took me longer to get the chair to climb on and the hanger to hook the keys with from the attendant in the Paradise Truck Stop than it did for me to get my keys out of the car. I went back in to get the soda I wanted in the first place and came out a few minutes later. The good news is I had definitely quit crying and just become kind of numb. The Kentucky game was still on when I started the car, and my mind was in a zombie kind of zone. They are playing way down in Louisiana...how am I getting the signal for this game from so far away? How did he know to hit the seek button just three times? I just kept asking myself, What is going on? as I started to pull out of the truck stop.

"Ann, one more thing...please. Turn your car around as you come out of here."

What? Oh, Gary, is this even possible? I don't think I can take this.

"Please, Annie, turn your car around."

After having my mind blown away by songs and football games, I didn't have anything left to argue with and I did as my "thoughts" told me to.

My thoughts? Oh, dear God...I turned my car around.

There was a typical farm field alongside the truck stop, and after turning my car around, it was now right in front of me. At the other end of this field was a grove of trees starting to adorn themselves in the fall's colors. From this distance, one of the sections of trees formed a V-shape, and right between those trees, the sun was five minutes from setting.

I just sat there, and watched and cried my way through one of the most beautiful sunsets I have ever experienced. And of all places, I was in the middle of nowhere in northern Indiana at the Paradise Truck Stop listening to UK take on LSU down in the Bayou.

And the thought came..."I love you, Annie...now you can go home."

The First Wave

The first wave soaked me
with the intimacy of déjà vu.
A magic that is haunting
was steeped in this lagoon.

In these wish-filled waters
I first had learned to swim;
floated in this place with trust.
Some memories never dim.

Waves cool and warm at once,
a dichotomy felt in pleasure;
opposites flowing into one
with a tingling that is treasure.

Bathed in fond remembrance
I dove deep within the past.
Time flooded then and now
needing both, for each to last.

Hypnotic waves caressed me
and whispered I wasn't alone.
I took refuge in these waters.
The current would lead me home.

*Dialogue of sound
surrounds communicating
messages from life.*

Chapter III
Cocooned in Yellow

Now, if I didn't tell anybody about pool games, I sure wasn't about to breathe a word of this weirdness to anyone. I just couldn't picture saying to someone, "Well, you see, I have this friend who died, and while I was by myself driving along the highway, he 'talked' to me through the radio."

That is the sound byte version of the chapter you just read, and to me, that was no different than telling someone I was from Mars and the CIA was out to get me. Who's going to believe that? I knew I wasn't from Mars nor was *any* government agency out to get me, and so did everyone else that knew me. When what you live sounds crazy, how does one speak out loud? Thinking that Gary had somehow used the radio to "talk" to me was CRAZY talk…stuff they put you away for. To me, it would be grounds for my husband to suggest I find a good therapist. I could see my friends shaking their heads at each other when they didn't think I was looking…tsk, tsk, tsk, it's such a shame. Maybe she is just going through the "change." Sounds a little melodramatic, I know, but that reaction was certainly more probable to me than to think that anyone would believe me.

In my life I started to get quiet. Thoughts swirled and at the same time just seemed to kind of hang in the air. I didn't know how to make what had happened unhappen…so I tried to ignore it, push it down, and keep it there. That can make one so busy trying to ignore something that the rest of their life doesn't have much to say.

A little over two months had passed since my trip to the Twilight Zone's radio world and it was January 1, 2001. New Year's Day was on a Monday that year and I won't soon forget it. The night before had been so promising. We had let loose with some very close friends for New Year's Eve and had a glorious time. On New Year's day we were still together at their home getting ready for brunch. Their cat, Parker, started acting very sick. He was dragging one of his back legs. I had not known these friends without Parker. They rushed him to an emergency animal clinic open that day and found out that he had had a stroke and there was nothing they could do for him. They returned home without Parker. He was gone. The tears started.

On Tuesday we found out that Martin's Uncle Will had also died on New Year's Day. He was my father-in-law's only brother and lived in Arizona. Uncle Will had suffered from diabetes for many years, and his body had finally given out. Martin's father had called to tell us, and asked if I would arrange to have some masses said for him. More tears fell.

On Wednesday the third I received a call from my mother that my brother John had been in a horrible car accident. The doctors thought he was going to be okay, but he was in intensive care and on a respirator and she would let me know.

The tears gushed. Three days of sadness, a triple whamee, if you will, progressing in strength as it rolled along.

On Thursday I was running around getting things taken care of so that I could get myself down south to the hospital. I had desperately wanted to go down on Wednesday as soon as I heard, but my mother said that things were, needless to say, crazy and there was nothing I could do for him by rushing down. They were only allowing Jacquelyn to see him, and that was limited. Mom suggested I get the care of my boys squared away and head down on Friday. If things got real bad, real fast, she would call me and then I could rush down. Sensible advice from a mom; I needed it and was finally old enough to take it. I ran around getting groceries bought, supplies stocked, calls made. I went to a church nearby and got a series of masses set up in Uncle Will's name. I knew if I let that go right now it wouldn't get done.

Friday afternoon Martin came home from work early and I got on the road. Two hours later I was pulling into the hospital-parking garage. I walked into the hospital from a tunnel on the second floor of the garage into the second floor of the hospital. I had his room number and knew that I could find my way. I have two boys that have always been, as my mother-in-law says, very busy boys. Between the two of them, they have had more than six broken bone "incidents," some with multiple broken bones—a couple requiring hospital stays, one lasting at least a week. I was no longer intimidated by entering a hospital. I realized before this was over, I would know my way around fairly well and didn't need to start by the front door.

I was walking along a corridor looking for the elevators, when I "just happened" to glance up and notice the chapel door. I walked on past and at the end of the hall, the thought "pops" in…Which comes first? I had to stop to think about that for a moment, and I literally did just that. I stopped walking and just stood for a moment.

My brother was still alive and just a couple of floors above me. This I knew. I had arrived safely and would see him in the next few minutes. John had been hit while driving on the expressway. His car was hit by a truck that had lost control and gone airborne after it had gone down into and then sailed out of the gully median that separated the west bound lanes from the east bound lanes of the expressway. The truck landed on the driver's side of my brother's car. John was driving and alone. What comes first?

Thanks, gratitude, respect for whatever had protected him and allowed me to be visiting the hospital and not the cemetery. I got it. I turned around and walked through the

29

door that read Chapel. This was a very humble space and I would soon find out just how powerful humble spaces can be. It was a non-denominational chapel and had a lovely banner hanging in the front with a simple altar. On that alter was one of the largest Bibles I have ever seen. I walked up to the altar and just looked up and said thanks. I opened the Bible somewhere in the middle to read a verse as my way of starting a prayer of deep thanks. I read the first paragraph at the top of the left page and I am sorry to say I can't remember what or where these verses were, but that is not important: the message was. Three times in the first passage it spoke of taking care of one's brother; not only the brother that is a sibling to you, but your fellow brothers in the world. That is not an unusual sentiment to find; it runs through the entire Bible like a river that everyone can come to the banks of and wade into. "Amen," I said. "Someone is watching over us...I am here to take care of my brother and I will do whatever I can to expand that. Thank you, God, for allowing John to be here."

Everything was so quiet: the room, my mind, the "thoughts," and a calmness seeped through me. In my little universe at that moment, everyone and everything took a deep breath. I headed out to find my brother and ten minutes later I was standing in front of him.

John had major trauma to the upper left part of his body. He had a broken scapula, clavicle, and ribs; his left lung had collapsed but was now working again with the help of a respirator attached to a tube that came out of his throat. It is very, very difficult to see anyone you love in a great deal of physical pain, and harder for the one in pain to see those he loves.

Jacquelyn had not left the hospital since Wednesday. Her mother Sophia, one of my all time favorite women, had flown in the night before. My sister Audrey and Jacquelyn's brother Stephen were both flying in from California, and my parents had gone to the airport to get them and bring them to the hospital. My sister Rachael and my brother-in-law Brad had left the hospital only to take care of anything and everything Jacquelyn needed or asked them to do. We all had, what I am sure you can understand, some very emotional days. But the family wagons had circled and we all drew strength from the power of that circle.

Later that evening my sister, Audrey, and Sophia took Jacquelyn to a hotel room a few blocks down from the hospital. Sophia had gotten two rooms: one for herself and anybody else that needed it, and one for Jacquelyn. Jacquelyn hadn't slept in over 48 hours, only napped; she hadn't changed clothes or seen much of their three kids. She needed to get out for a while, but not alone. So Sophia, Stephen, and Audrey took her to the hotel until the morning. Rachel and Brad went home to see their own kids and to try to get some rest after days of very little. My parents left to visit with John and Jacquelyn's kids and tell them their dad was doing okay, and then they were headed home for some sleep.

That night for me was about trying to keep John as comfortable as possible and my learning the routine of the nurses who were taking wonderful care of him. I was there to give him love, support, a hand to hold, and to try to be backup when the nurses couldn't understand what he wanted. Brothers and sisters can communicate in a language without speaking. If you have one of those types of relationship with a brother or a sister, you are very lucky and indeed blessed. I am both.

John was restless with pain, but I did manage to get a nap in during the night. Jacquelyn was back before dawn on Saturday looking at least more rested. She had lots of doctors to meet with, and she wanted at least to try to have a meal with the kids at some point. People came and went all day. They couldn't get in to see John because, understandably, ICU allowed only one person in his room at a time and that was for immediate family only; but that did not stop a constant stream of love from pouring onto that hospital floor. Friends and family were constantly coming and going.

I stayed at the hospital all day. Coffee, Cokes, and worried energy for John kept us all going. Saturday evening, Jacquelyn and my sister Audrey left to go visit the kids and put them to bed. They were then going to the hotel to be close to the hospital and try to get another night's sleep. I stayed with John. I was going to have to go back home to Indy the next day for at least the week to take care of my brood, and I didn't need or want to leave the hospital before I had to. The doctors had changed John's pain medication somewhat and it helped him rest much better.

Sometime around midnight, I was getting myself tucked into a chair for sleeping. It was a reclining chair so you could push the back down somewhat, and I was trying to get comfortable, when some bells and whistles started to go off around John.

The nurse immediately came into the room. The tube attached to the respirator machine had slid off the connecting tube in John's neck and that had set off the buzzers. I watched what the nurse did and then she said, "He's fine, just that tube coming loose. Try to get some rest while you can." And off she went to take care of her other patients. So I settled back into the chair and tried to do as she said.

The paramedic who had originally treated John at the scene of the accident had tried to put a breathing tube down John's throat. He tried three times, but couldn't get the tube to go down all the way. John started turning blue and the paramedic saved his life by cutting into John's neck and inserting a trachea tube into the center of his neck. That is why John still had the respirator tube connected to the outside of his neck.

I was just heading into sleep when the buzzer went off again, and this time I'm up putting the tube back into place as the nurse walks in. She shut off the buzzer and headed back out. I lay back down and began the getting-to-sleep process again. By the time the buzzers had gone off four times, I realized the tube was sometimes popping loose when John deeply exhaled. Not every time, but every 15 to 20 minutes the tube would just "pop" again. John's nurse said that the tube and the connector in his neck needed cleaning, but that no one would be around to do that until the doctor in charge of his respiration and breathing came in sometime after 7:00 a.m. She said she was glad I was there. If I hadn't been there, the buzzer would be going off all night and that would make John's night even rougher. By this time it was around 2:00 a.m., and I knew I wasn't going to get any sleep.

Trying to get to sleep, only to be woken by a loud noise over and over again, would give me an awful headache and I really didn't want that to happen. So I realized I had an "all-nighter" to do, and quite frankly, that was okay by me. I have had my share of all-nighters in my life, for a variety of reasons: finals, parties, having babies, taking care of those babies. Staying up all night for my brother or any friend or family member, for that matter, is something I would do many times over, regardless of reason. But what do I do with myself without turning on lights that might disturb John?

Gary, are you there? I thought to myself, and I had to smile.

I was starting to admit to myself that "Something" was somehow always around, watching over all of us. The "coincidences" were just too amazing not to at least wonder about them. So I decided to initiate a dialogue with the empty room surrounding me. Having John so hurt in that hospital bed certainly motivated me to reach out to anything that might be there, and I was more than willing to try to believe whatever "thoughts" came into my head if it would help in any way.

My brother and I had two grandfathers and one grandmother who had died. We had three great-aunts that were very, very special to us who were also "gone." Jacquelyn had a grandfather and a very special Nana that had "passed." I had started to think maybe, just maybe, they were in that room with John and me. If so, it was a crowded room, indeed. A thought came into my head and I felt like it was my grandma. She asked a question, "Would any of us be anywhere else, Ann? If there was nothing to stop us, where would we be, if not right here by his side?" At that point I didn't care whether it was just wishful thinking on my part that put these thoughts into my head or not. A conversation with myself would at least keep me from feeling sleepy for a while.

Okay, I thought to the Unseen in the room, I find myself with nothing to do but try to stay awake. Please tell me what I can do to help him in some way and help myself stay up all night. What prayers can I say? Do I meditate? How do I do that? Any of you have any ideas?

The thought comes back, "Put your hands out over John's chest."

And I think, Oh, yeah, right...I can't do that.

"Why not? You just said you had nothing better to do."

Well, yes I did, but I feel silly.

"You are being silly, but not in the way that you think. Who's to care if you look silly? What have you got to lose except time, and it seems to me you have plenty of that on your hands...Pun fully intended."

I had to laugh and I realized there was no argument to that. So I put my hands out and thought, Now what?

"Think yellow."

Yellow?...*Yellow?*...Are you kidding? What's yellow got to do with anything? I don't even like the color yellow.

"Ann, think of all the wondrous things that have been created for you in your world that are yellow. Think of some that represent healing and warmth to you. John had a collapsed lung; he still has broken ribs, broken scapula, and a trachea tube. It is very important that he not go into pneumonia. Right now he has a lot of gunk in his chest that needs to be melted slowly, like warm butter... yellow... healing... warmth...can you do that?"

Okay, wondrous things created for me yellow...warmth, healing...the sun! I can think about the warmth and healing power of the sun...I can do this. So I proceed to put my hands out over the area most hurt on John and I think about the sun. I think about our summer vacations at Lake Michigan when we were kids. I thought about all the afternoons with our kids in his backyard or mine. I thought about all the great times under the sun I know he and Jacquelyn had on the beaches of California while they were living there. I thought...and thought...and thought.

After a while I started to get very warm, which happens to anyone if they sit thinking about the sun for any length of time, and that easily led to my getting sleepy. John was quieter. The tube hadn't popped for quite awhile. I thought I might be able to get in a nap after all. So I went back to the chair and tried to settle in. A couple of minutes later, the buzzers went off again.

I got up and plugged the tube back in, shut off the alarms and then the thought comes into my head, "We're not done with you yet. Come on back over here where you were."

Really? Okay, but I've been thinking a lot about the sun, and quite frankly, I'm a little burned out on that...pun fully intended to you!

"Touché," I hear, and then the thought comes, "Annie, you have a passion for flowers and your gardens. Think of all the yellow flowers that represent healing and strength to you."

Flowers? Now you want me to think about yellow flowers? I don't see how this will help John at all, but as we all agree, I've got nothing better to do. So I put my hands out and I started to think of yellow flowers that would represent healing and strength. I had been thinking about the sun, and it is a very small step to sunflowers. By this time, it was somewhere between 3:00 and 4:00 in the morning, and I wasn't in any mood to "think" too hard about anything. But I thought about sunflowers. And the more I thought about them, the stronger I seemed to become. Sunflower seeds aren't even the size of a dime, but in sixty days they can reach over eight feet. Think of that. If nothing else, the power in the genetics involved gives one pause.

The very dear friends who had lost their cat Parker on New Year's Day had grown the most glorious sunflowers that past summer. They had regally towered above us all. In infinite shades of yellow to gold, they stood in the sun. Sunflowers seem to be created to look as if paying homage to the image of the sun itself, giving the flower its name. I thought about sunflowers until I was "thought out" of sunflowers. And then, of all things, this image of a field of goldenrod popped into my head. I thought about driving down the highway when we were kids, wondering if the trip would ever end. Then you would see a field of solid yellow driving along, and you couldn't help but smile. As I got older, I realized most people in my area of the world thought goldenrod was little more than a weed and the main cause of my mother's hay fever, but still it made me smile. That, I decided, was how I liked yellow best...just a huge area of yellow speckled with green in some field somewhere along my way.

About this time, I look up at the clock and realize that it is 5:00 in the morning. I knew from past experiences that I had made it through the all-nighter. Anyone who has stayed up all night realizes that if you make it to 5 a.m. and can get a cup of coffee, maybe go for a little walk, you have made it through the night. John was sleeping as soundly as he could, and his breathing had gotten quieter. The tube hadn't popped in about an hour and the nurses' shift change was coming, which meant more of them would be around to handle bells and whistles. The coffee and short walk is exactly what I did. Jacquelyn was there soon after I got back to John's room and Sunday morning was beginning.

***

A couple hours later everybody was back at the hospital and I headed to my parents' home for a shower and a nap. I knew I was going to be driving home later that night and I needed a little rest. I slept on one of their couches for about three hours before the phone rang. A family friend had called at Mom and Dad's to see how John was doing. It was time to get up. I took a shower and headed back to the hospital about noon.

One of my mother's sisters, my Aunt Geri, and her daughter, my cousin Sheryl, had driven down from Indianapolis for the day to check on John. Sheryl is a registered nurse who works in surgical recovery at a hospital in Indy. She wanted to see how John was, talk to the nurses herself to see how he was "really" doing, and help Jacquelyn any way she could. It was wonderful having them there.

I went into John's room and Sheryl was standing over him while he was sleeping. "Hi," she whispered. "Come on in. I was just doing some laying on of hands to help his healing. I was thinking about him on a summer's day playing with the kids in his yard, the sun beating down, all of them bored to death and what a great day that will be."

I didn't say a word. I just stood there looking at her.

She continued, "All that thinking about hot summer days under the sun has got me burning up and I need to get out of here. Why don't you try, it certainly won't hurt him. Give me your hands." She took my hands and poured a little water into them from a container she had sitting there. "This is Holy Water," she said. "Mom got it at a little chapel next to the ocean the last time she was in Ireland. Now put your hands out over him and just say a prayer." And out of the room she walked.

I hadn't said a word the entire time she was in there. I had started to tell her about my thinking about the sun not a few hours before, but she was already headed out. There was nothing for me to do but pick up where she left off and I thought to myself, if I'm crazy, I'm not alone, and for a few more minutes, my hands went out over John. I wondered what might bloom yellow along the Irish coastline....

***

Around 6:00 that evening it was time for me to head home to Indy. Aunt Geri and Sheryl had left a couple hours before because Indianapolis had a few inches of snow on the ground from the week before and more was expected. I didn't want to leave but there wasn't anything I could really do about it. The next day was Monday and I had work, the boys had school. I was coming back down the next weekend, but I needed to get going now before it got to be too late. I gave my hugs, said my good-byes, and reluctantly headed to the parking garage.

I took the path out of the hospital that I had taken coming in two days ago and walked through the hallway with the chapel. This time I went in to say my thanks. That I might be driving into snow added a little incentive.

As I walked up to the center table, I noticed the Bible was already opened far to the back. This Book was one of the largest I had ever seen, and it being open with only a small part left on the right side made me pause to take a look at where it had been left open. It was the beginning of the Second Letter of Paul to Timothy.

The week before John's accident, a day before New Year's Eve, I had finished reading a book by Gore Vidal entitled *Live From Golgotha*. I have enjoyed many of his books over the years. This one was an unusual subject, even for Gore Vidal. The premise of the book is that the major news networks have discovered a way to travel back in time and they are racing each other to see who can be the first to film the Crucifixion, live and in Technicolor. It was, at the very least, a unique plot, and the story was told through the eyes of Saint Timothy. Much of Timothy's narrative was the telling of his traveling adventures with Saint Paul. The story was told in a style that could be woven only by Mr. Vidal.

I looked down at this exquisitely huge Bible and saw the Second Letter of Paul to Timothy and I thought to myself, This is TOO weird. I feel as if I somehow know you two. Within the first few verses I read (2 Timothy 1:6-7), *Hence I remind you to rekindle the gift of God that is within you through the laying on of my hands; for God did not give us a spirit of timidity but a spirit of power and love and self-control.*

And I let out this very quiet, "Woooewww." It is the first time I remember raising one of my arms straight up over my head as a sign of thanks to God. I have no idea why I did it except that it seemed the natural thing to do. It wasn't to be the last time. Needless to say, that particular passage in the Bible gave me a wonderful energy boost as I headed to the car for my drive home, feeling better than I had in over a week.

***

The next morning was Monday, January 8. It had been a week since New Year's Day when this saga seemed to have begun. We had gotten snow during the night but not too much, and I had made it home just fine. That morning was the boys' first morning back to school after Christmas break, and even though we had over four inches collected on the ground, the roads weren't bad and off they went to school.

I had a hard time getting into the work groove that morning for obvious reasons. I am a freelance graphic designer who has a studio set up in our home. Graphic design allows me to work a job and still be home when the boys get off the bus. I have my in-laws to thank for this treasure, and it is a gift I can never repay. It certainly has been a blessing for their grandsons to have "mommy" around, even though she is working. They had started the studio years before and brought me in when I moved to Indy. I try to pay back my gratitude by raising their grandsons in a way that hopefully will make them proud.

On this particular morning, my head and heart were still down in Louisville with my brother and everyone else. But there were ads to put together, jobs backed up that were supposed to have been ready last week, bills to pay, the house to straighten, and I was trying to get what I could done. That afternoon there was a knock at my kitchen door. It was my Aunt Geri all bundled up, trying to stay warm and carrying what seemed like all kinds of things in one big heap. I opened the back door and told her to come on in. "Oh, no," she said, "I have to get back to my house. My grandchildren will be home soon and I am watching them today when they get off the bus. I just wanted you to know that I love you and was thinking of you and wanted to bring you and the boys a few things. John is going to be okay!" She proceeded to turn this bundle of stuff over to me and headed for her car.

"Aunt Geri, I love you. Thank you so much for thinking of me today," I said, "Surely you can stay for a moment." But she was already half-way to the car and off she went. Everyone should have an Aunt Geri in their life, absolutely everyone…the love…but that is a story for another time.

I came into the kitchen and put down a bag of fancy cookies for the boys, a card of encouragement for me, and opened the largest of the wrapped bundles. What happened next I can never forget or return from. The largest bundle was a bouquet of flowers...solid yellow. There were no purple flowers, no blue, no white, no red, no pink, no other color...nothing but yellow and there were only three kinds of flowers in this bouquet: sunflowers, goldenrod, and roses....

I dropped to my knees in the middle of my kitchen floor and cried like a baby.

What was I supposed to do with that "little" coincidence? What would you have done? What would you think? There were over four inches of snow on the ground, it was the eighth of January, and I was holding solid yellow. And not just any flowers of yellow...oh no, I was holding only sunflowers...goldenrod...and as a final, some might say perfect, touch—three yellow roses. I finally picked myself up off the floor, put the flowers in a vase, and sat them on the counter. Then, quite honestly, I sat back down in the middle of the floor and cried a little more.

"You're for real," I said to the Unseen in the empty room around me.

"Yep," I heard in my thoughts.

"Oh, my God...."

"Say that again, and realize this time what you are saying."

I started to do something else I had been raised to do, which was to make the sign of the cross, and that was something I rarely did anymore. I remember this moment as a kind of "movie moment" in my life and I was being very dramatic; some would say melodramatic, I grant you, but my life was being melodramatic.

I started to make the sign of the cross and in my thoughts I hear, "Let me tell you how it was originally done. Humans tend to shorten things over time, create shortcuts, do things

41

faster, easier. However, that does not always mean better; the full meaning of things can be lost when shortcuts happen. If everyone today did what was originally done a couple thousand years ago, the world would have a little better understanding of who they really are. When you make the sign of the cross this time, leave your right hand on your left shoulder and then bring your left hand up to your right shoulder and see if you have a little more clarity about you and a Holy Spirit." The tears bathed me as I became cocooned in yellow.

A Coincidence Maze

The 1st time it happened,
I was a mazed.

The 2d time it happened,
I stood dazed.

The 3d time it happened,
my foundations hazed.

The 8th time it happened,
a mind gone crazed?

The 10th time it happened
to the heavens I gazed.

Chaos in order
forms a metamorphosis.
Signals in the dark.

Chapter IV
Deep Breathing in Stasis

This chapter will seem a little disjointed, but that describes my life perfectly around this time. It is one of the feelings you experience while being cocooned and having who you thought you were changed into something you had no idea you could be. There is confusion and lots of deep breathing when you don't know if you are coming or going. Ask any caterpillar what it feels like morphing in their cocoon. They will tell you: joints they didn't know they had are taken apart and put back together again.

At this point you may need to know a little more about my background before you go any further down this path with me, and I can't say as I blame you. With the direction you can see this dialogue headed in, I should tie up some "loose ends" about my "faith" and how it was shaped as I was growing up.

I am first generation Irish on my mother's side, and that alone might tell you that odds are, I was raised Catholic. My dad was born in Kentucky and raised Catholic as well, and that would clinch it. My parents were and are very sincere in their faith and I deeply respect and admire that. I am not writing this in an attempt at another bashing of Catholicism or *any* faith. This is about something quite different.

Much of my disillusionment with a God and any church came about simply through the rebelliousness of youth. I have known many devoted priests, nuns, ministers, men and women of deep faith, of many different religions, who were loving, kind, devout, and sincere. My mother's second sister, my Aunt Helena, had started the family's migration to the

44

states because of her deep desire to become a nun. She is a very intelligent, warm, and generous woman who traveled to St. Mary's College in South Bend, Indiana at the age of 16 to enter the convent.

By the time I was 16, I had gone in the opposite direction. Something inside of me changed when I became a teenager, with regards to my personal perspectives toward the Catholic Church in particular, and all institutionalized religions, in general. By the time of Gary's death I had, in many ways, turned my back on any church, and I had done it many years before, for many reasons. I had a problem early on with the hypocrisy I saw in religion in general: Do unto others as long as they believe the way you believe, is what I saw most people do in this world. Churches, ministries, synagogues, etc., seemed to rest very strongly on the "you're either with us or against us" kind of philosophy. Unfortunately for the world today, many still do. I never did believe that God would wish it to be this way. There are over 1,100 species of butterflies and each is perfect in its own way. Why would there be only one correct way to worship and believe in God?

No authority in the Catholic Church EVER physically abused me; however, I was verbally chewed out by a very sad, old priest. He was the pastor of the church my family attended and a Monsignor in "rank." I was thirteen and very impressionable, and like most girls of that age, very emotional as well. I cried for three days after he chewed me out in his office for suggesting that my eighth grade class have a dance in the cafeteria to celebrate our graduation from our school. There had never been a dance for the kids at our school, and he certainly wasn't going to allow a change in that rule under his "management." The Monsignor saying no wasn't the problem. All the eighth graders expected the idea to be turned down, including me. The problem was the verbal assault he subjected me to during our meeting. To this day, I do not understand why he felt he had the right to talk to a young girl the way he did, full of anger and cruel words. He referred to me more than once as "a very loose type of girly he might have to marry off quick. You girls wanting parties are just that type."

Now in my life at that time, I had made sure I was in no way "a loose type of girly" Actually I feel very safe in saying that no one else that knew me then thought I was in anyway "loose" either. I had never been spoken to that abusively and with so little civility before. I decided that if this judgmental, mean-spirited old guy was the type of man God wanted as a symbol of Godliness, then maybe I didn't want to have much to do with a God and "His Church."

The good news was that my parents were so upset by the verbal tirade he subjected me to that they and several other sets of parents made sure that my eighth grade class got our "dance" in the cafeteria. It was a wonderful night for all the kids in my class and me that year.

However, I never related my disconnected feelings toward God and "His Religions" to my parents. I still grudgingly went to church and did what I was told. But inside of my own mind I had wondered if God was so powerful, so omnipotent, then why would He allow mean and ugly people to be in positions of authority in any of His churches? I decided He wouldn't, so maybe there wasn't a God. Perhaps these were very juvenile and naïve feelings, but they were very real to me and would continue to affect my attitudes for many years to come. Over time, as I had more control over what I did with my life, I went to church less and less. I did get married in the church I was raised in and we had our sons baptized in a church, more out of respect for our sons' grandparents on both sides than because of some deep belief my husband and I had, or because it was something we felt God required of us. I felt a belief in a "Higher Being" was very much an intellectual exercise of the mind, and I didn't go out of my way to strengthen any knowledge or faith in much of anything. Did I believe "something" was there? Yes, I would have to say, deep down, I always at least hoped "something" was out there…some kind of version of Heaven where we could finally relax and have a great time with everyone after we "arrived." I did have hope…I had started the conversations with Gary in my head on at least hope. Now things had changed for me and changed in a big way. If Gary and others are still "around" in some way, what did that mean for me?…What do I do now?

***

You cannot undo events in your life; you cannot unknow something once it has been experienced. A caterpillar cannot undo the process, once started. I had now experienced too many alarm clocks going off to hit the snooze button and think I could go back to sleep…I decided it was time for me to start saying something out loud about all of this to someone. At that moment, with a vase of yellow staring me in the face, the logical place for me to start looking for answers was with my Aunt Geri. She was, after all, the "giver" of this bouquet of yellow splendor. Why did she bring these particular flowers to me? What was going on?

I mentioned earlier that everyone should have an Aunt Geri. She is one of my mother's sisters. After their younger sister Helena traveled to the States, Geri and my mother decided to come as well. They both married in the same year. I was my parents' first child and was born the same year my Aunt Geri and Uncle Frank had their first-born son. My parents had my brother the following year; Aunt Geri and her husband had their second during the next year. It goes on like that until both families have four children: three girls and one boy for each.

There have always been many things I loved about Geri while I was growing up. One is that she has always spoken aloud about her dreams. She has sensed things were going to happen. She dreams about people and the circumstances they are in and gets in touch with them to check and see if they are okay. Often something would have happened to them. Sometimes the news was good, sometimes it was bad, but if it was a big event in their lives, Geri seemed to know it was coming before they did. I had always thought it had something to do with being a very in-tuned, red-headed Irish woman. I love her dearly.

I waited for an hour to pass before I called her. I knew she would be home by then and I needed to know why she...how she?...I just knew I needed to talk to her. Had she had one of her "dreams" about me? What had possessed her to bring over these particular flowers to me? That is exactly what I asked her when she answered the phone.

Her reply?

"Oh, honey, I woke up this morning and thought you needed a big bouquet of yellow daffodils. Spring will get here soon enough and John will be much better by then. You have such wonderful daffodils blooming in the spring and I thought if I could find you some it would cheer you up. I looked in every flower shop between my house and yours and it is just too early for daffodils. I had given up and gone to the grocery to get a few things. As I walk into the store there was this beautiful bouquet of yellow and I knew it was perfect for you. So, I picked out a card, got some cookies for the boys, and brought it all over to you."

I started to tell her about the flowers and what had been in my "head" less than 48 hours before, but I was still very emotional and it kind of came out in "fits and starts." I was having a hard time being calm and coherent about what had happened to me at the hospital. I realized I still wasn't able to explain it all out loud. I thanked her profusely for giving me such a fantastic bouquet of yellow flowers, in the beginning of January no less. I assured her that daffodils wouldn't have "cheered me up" nearly as much as these flowers had and I got off the phone.

The boys were going to be home from school soon and I needed to get myself together, which I did. But I must admit I found myself spending a lot of time in the kitchen during the rest of the day just looking at a vase flowing over in yellow.

***

That night I started to talk to my husband about what had happened and what I had "thought" in my head in John's room at the hospital, but I still couldn't phrase it well. I started to tell him the story after dinner, but the boys had homework questions to be answered and I figured we would talk later. After a few hours we had the boys in bed and I thought about bringing up the subject again, but I just didn't. I was emotionally drained from the day, from the weekend before, and I just wanted to go to sleep.

The next morning the boys were off to school and Martin was off to work. I still hadn't said much to anybody and I knew I needed to talk. Late in the morning I called Susan, the Spiritualist minister that worked at the same firm as my husband. I was able to get the story out to her in just a few minutes while she patiently listened. She said, "What a beautiful confirmation." My jaw dropped on the other end of the line and I asked her to repeat what she said. She said, "Annie, many times when our spirit guides talk to us, they will send proof in some way. We call that 'confirmation.' The flowers are your confirmation that you were indeed heard and spoken to. Don't you think?"

I told her that I was sure she was right and what a beautiful way of saying it. I thanked her for being there and listening to my ramblings and got off the phone. She had no idea at the time what the word "confirmation" would do to me. That word to someone raised Catholic brings back memories of their "Confirmation" ceremony. As with many old religions, there is a ceremony for just about everything. Through the sacrament of Confirmation, it is said the person is perfectly bound to the Church and enriched with a special strength of the Holy Spirit. A Confirmation ceremony under Catholic dogma "seals you" with the gift of the "Holy Spirit."

The Catholic Church's Confirmation Ceremony is usually a "rite" you go through around the age of 12 to 13. Each teen is asked to pick a sponsor who isn't a parent to walk down the aisle at church with them for this particular ceremony. My Confirmation sponsor when I was 13 was my Aunt Geri.

Now, I was 42 and many, many miles away from that time. It seemed the Unseen had chosen Aunt Geri to be my Confirmation sponsor yet again.

***

A week later it was time for the first mass being said in Uncle Will's memory at a Catholic church near my home. Remember him? He was my father-in-law's brother who had died New Year's Day and I had arranged for masses to be said for him. It was now a little over two weeks since my brother's accident.

I attended the first mass with about eight other adults. It was the first time I had been in a Catholic Church in over a year. The priest was very friendly and social. He spoke to each of us before the service and asked who I was because he didn't recognize me. I told him my name and he said, "This mass is being said for a member of your family." I told him about Uncle Will; he thanked me for being there and started the service.

The first reading that day was from the First Letter of St. Paul to the Corinthians. St. Paul again...I heard that and thought to myself, Well, of course it is.

And the priest started to read, "To each individual the manifestation of the Holy Spirit is given for some benefit. To one is given the expression of wisdom; to another the expression of knowledge according to the same Spirit; to another faith by the same Spirit; to another gifts of healing by the one Spirit; to another mighty deeds; to another prophecy; to another discernment of spirits; to another varieties of tongues; to another interpretation of tongues. But one and the same Spirit produces all of these, distributing them individually to each person as he wishes..." (1 Corinthians 12:7-11)

And in spite of myself, I hear my own thoughts speak up inside my head..."Uncle Will, you there?"

He was.

Presence Reflected

Particled images
are always around,
from forested shadows
to rocks on the ground.
In all that surrounds us
their sketches are found.

Subtle portraits are
ingeniously drawn
for Nature illustrates
those who have gone.
In all that surrounds us
remembrance is strong.

Tides in life
form waves of sound;
from each Given moment
the messages profound.
In all that surrounds us
the Dialogue resounds.

Awareness of patterns
changes perspective,
regardless of setting
the dots are connected.
In all that surrounds us
their presence reflected.

*Growing pains provide
the necessary struggle
needed to evolve.*

Chapter V
It's Dark in Here and I'm Scared...

I could run. I could walk. I could crawl...I couldn't hide.
I ask you, where was there for me to go? I worried that
everything was going to start spinning out of control because
I certainly didn't think I had any. Spirits, spiritualism, Holy
Spirit...holy ghost was more accurate. I felt in a way like I
was caught in some kind of energy whirlwind I didn't have a
clue how to control..."*Holy ghost, Batman, how do we make
it stop?*" That may sound ridiculous to most people and
downright sacrilegious to the rest, but I don't know where I
would have been at this time in my life without humor, even
very bad humor. If I hadn't laughed at myself a few times in
the midst of all this, I might have lost complete emotional
control and taken a nose dive into a deep depression. Some
"little thing," some type of "coincidence" happened daily
with the invisible world that I was beginning to see
surrounding me and much of it seemed psychotic. A running
dialogue from the words in music and what seemed to be
random phrases from any and all media communicated love,
answers, and even jokes about events in my life anywhere
and everywhere I went. I was beginning to wonder if I was
losing a grip on reality, and I still couldn't bring myself to
talk to anybody about any of this because everything seemed
so profoundly personal. I realize now that this is an
exquisitely unique and emotionally charged roller coaster ride
for everyone. Metamorphosis, as with any birth, starts by
turning you upside down.

There are many butterflies in this world and the wing
pattern on any two of us is never alike, for the same reason no

two snowflakes are ever alike: it isn't possible. Snowflakes, like butterflies, are created...not duplicated...one at a time.

I didn't realize I was going to be meeting other butterflies, but they were going to show up in a variety of ways to help get me through this journey. Quite a few would fly through my life to help me see what it was like to make it to the other side of the cocoon. Two butterflies that helped me at this time were the newly graduated Spiritualist minister, Reverend Susan Hill, and her partner, the Reverend Mike Mellott. Susan at this time worked for the same company as my husband. Once a month, Susan and Mike held an evening class to talk about "spirits" that assist us from the other side if and when you train yourself to listen. Okay, I thought, I'm listening. I started going to their meetings. I couldn't bring myself to say much to either of them about everything that had been going on, but I did relate the story of receiving a bouquet of yellow splendor, and to me that was plenty.

During one of their classes, Mike explained something in a way that would affect me tremendously. He was explaining different ways of receiving "messages" and what could block a person from receiving them. He told us that, "If you are coming from your highest place of Love and Light, the first second of receiving a message is Truth; the next second is your humanness doubting that truth; and the third second is you talking yourself out of believing the message you were given. You must stop yourself from believing the doubt you yourself create in the second and third seconds and HOLD ON to the Truth given to you in the first second." I have never forgotten his wisdom and it has served me well so many times in so many ways. So many people have a tendency to jump from Truth, Happiness, Joy into negative thoughts without missing a beat. Why?

Another person I told about the yellow bouquet is one of my dearest friends. Her name is Jan and I have known her since I first started dating Martin. She and I have been close ever since. She invited me to what she called a Psychic Thursday evening. Another dear friend of mine, Alice, and Jan have a group of girlfriends who get together a couple evenings a year for cocktails, munchies, and fun. They call these evenings "Psychic Thursday" parties. It is obvious what night of the week these soirées are held on and as the name implies, you can also enjoy a little psychic reading of some kind during the evening if you wish. One time there might be a palmist, another time a Tarot card reader. Once we had a medium that communicated with spirits, a woman reading coffee grounds, and a manicurist, all in the same evening. Talk about conversations being "stimulating and spirited." These evenings are a great deal of fun, very healing, and wonderfully therapeutic for all the women that attend. Psychic Thursdays usually occur at least twice a year, around Halloween and once again around St. Patrick's Day. I had started attending these Psychic Thursdays the March gathering after Gary "died." It was March again, and my third time enjoying a Psychic Thursday party. That night we had a Tarot card reader to enjoy.

At this point I was starting to get into the "Unseen" in my world a great deal more than I would have admitted to many, and by that I do mean I started getting "in to it."

...in to it

...in tu it

...intuit

...intuitive...See how that works? It is said by many that parents and particularly mothers are intuitive when it comes to their children. Well, of course they are. Parents get very "in to it" when "it" has anything to do with their children. They therefore can be very intuitive about their children.

New ideas "popped" in all the time. Conversations in my thoughts went back and forth as I tried to keep some kind of control on my fears. I thought I was being shown that I was supposed to start working on healing in some way. I hoped the Tarot reader at this particular Psychic Thursday evening would give me some kind of direction as to how that might happen. It had been just a few weeks since I had received the yellow flowers and I was still spending a great deal of time just thinking about the events that had occurred: wondering, worrying about what it all meant. I should have just been joyous at the special Hello I had received and celebrated that fact, but I wasn't looking at things like a butterfly...just flying around...not just yet. I was in the middle of my cocoon and worried about what "in the hell" was going on, and what I got that evening was a reading that scared the "holy shiitake" out me.

Remember when you were a kid and you were crying about something silly and some adult would say, "You stop crying right now or I will give you something to really cry about"? Well, I had been worrying about things that had happened instead of being thrilled and happy about it all. So on this particular evening, I was given something to truly cry about.

***

A man named Mark was one of the mediums giving Tarot readings at this particular Psychic Thursday evening. When it was your turn, you went in to Jan's guest bedroom, paid your money, and sat down. I had never seen him before. As I am writing this, I have not seen him since but I know that will change somewhere in the future. Mark was shuffling the cards as I sat down across from him at a small table. He handed me this huge deck of cards, asked me to cut them, and then proceeded to turn each card over and lay them down, one on top of another, in several vertical stacks until every card in this huge deck had been turned face up and was laying on the table. At the time, I had very little experience or knowledge with Tarot cards and didn't really know what they looked like or what any of them meant.

He looked up at me and said, "You are about to feel like the rug is being pulled out from under you, but it will be okay. This is a sacrifice you are willing to go through...."

I know my eyes blinked several times and I swallowed very hard as I said, "Excuse me, what did you just say, a sacrifice?" And my mind is thinking, I can't take much more; please tell me he didn't just say everything is about to get worse?

He takes another look at the cards and says, "Your main cards are the Tower card," which he points to, "and the Hanged Man card," which was next to it, "and you are about to have your foundations crumble around you, but it is something you *want* to have happen." My heart seemed to crumble and my mind screamed out, NO, I DON'T *WANT* IT TO HAPPEN!! Mark said a few other things to me about my kids and I started to get really scared. He started asking about vehicles and what I drove, and then I got more than scared; I got terrified...foundations crumbling...send a mother's intuition into fear about one of her kids getting hurt in a car and watch foundations crumble.

I finally looked straight at him and said, "Wait a minute. I have been given what I believe were some pretty strong signals that I am supposed to help in healing with my hands." I stuck both my hands out in front of him with the palms up and continued, "Surely there is something in those cards about me and healing? I don't understand what you are saying."

Mark looked at my hands and said, "I have no doubt that at some point you will help people through healing, but you must get through this first. Afterwards, if you still want to learn about healing work, I and many others will be happy to help you." I asked him how long this "foundation crumbling" business was supposed to go on. He thought I would be

57

through most of it in the next couple of months, certainly by the end of May.

Out of the bedroom I went with dread running through me. Something was going to happen in the next 60 days that was going to...what? I had no definite idea of what direction it would come from or what kind of turmoil was headed my way.

Yeah, well, I'm a mom and I felt like something really bad was going to happen and that had to mean it had something to do with my kids...but what? I left the party not long after my reading and drove home crying. I didn't sleep much that night, not much at all. The next morning I woke up and got the boys to school. It was a Friday and I remembered that a shop not far from where I lived called New Age People gave "readings" on Fridays. I called when they opened and found out that if I came in that morning, they would have someone there to give me a "reading." I had never gone in search of a reading like this before, but I felt that on some level I had been given a terrible diagnosis and I jumped at the chance for a "second" opinion.

***

Kevin was the gentleman giving "readings" that morning at the store and I had never met him before, either. I have spent more time with him since and he is a wondrous young man. We sat in a room that was on the second floor of New Age People while Kevin shuffled his cards in front of me and then asked me to cut them. When he started to lay them down, I realized they were very different cards from what I had seen the night before. These cards were composed of black and white line drawings on white cards and were very unique. I told him I hadn't seen cards like his before and he said that he had drawn them himself. He had worked for many years healing young kids and had created his drawings because they didn't scare kids nearly as much as the cards most people used as Tarot cards. Kevin also laid down his cards in a different configuration than Mark had the night before.

He began, "You are in for a difficult time; your foundations are going to be rocked, but this is something you want to have happen."

There must have been fear all over my face, for he looked up at me and quickly added, "It is going to be okay." I looked at him and at the time I didn't know why, but I pointed at one of the cards closest to me and asked, "What card is that?"

He replied, "That is my version of the Tower Card."

I looked at the card next to it and asked, "And that?"

He said, "It is the Hanged Man."

The same cards had appeared.

They didn't look like the same cards. It wasn't the same day, the same place, or the same person, but I was getting the same reading...same second opinion...ah, *#@*&%....now what?

I asked Kevin, "How long is it going to take for my 'foundations to be rocked'?"

He replied that the worst would be over by the end of June.

Great, I thought to myself, I just had 30 more days added on to my sentence. I had gone from the end of May the night before to the end of June now before this "ordeal" was going to be over, and I still had no idea what either of them were talking about. I asked him if he could give me specifics and he said, "No," and added that some events we just have to get to the other side of, and knowing about it ahead of time might change things that shouldn't be changed.

After my session with Kevin was over, I went back out into the store, bought my own pack of what is referred to as Rider-Waite Tarot®[1] cards, and a book that supposedly told me all I would need to begin to understand Tarot.

Physician, heal thyself.

When I got home from the store, the first thing I did was open the deck of cards and set the book next to me. I had been told that the Rider-Waite Tarot® cards are the style of cards that are most often used by Tarot readers. There are hundreds, if not thousands, of fortune telling cards, but these are the type most people recognize if they have ever heard of Tarot, and they were the brand of cards Mark had used at the Psychic Thursday party.

I searched through the deck for "The Tower" and "The Hanged Man" cards. Those words are imprinted on the cards, although I hadn't noticed that the night Mark had laid them out. I hadn't thought there would be any reason to pay particular attention to them when I was sitting there. It wasn't until I had left the room that all Mark had said to me started to sink in, so the first thing I wanted to do was to really get a good look at both these images.

The look of The Tower card is enough to scare anyone, and when you put it up next to The Hanged Man, I could see why these pictures could scare adults and certainly kids.

The book I had purchased showed pictures of this card and a few different styles of Tarot's The Tower card, also known as The Falling Tower or The Tower of Destruction. Great, I thought to myself, this really helps me feel more secure. I kept reading and it kept getting worse. Evidently, the lightening around The Tower on the card might represent the anger of God and the card usually shows bodies falling to their death. It is the 16th card of the Major Arcana, which meant that it symbolized and usually represented a big event in your life. It can represent the possibility that the foundations you have built your world on are about to be destroyed for one of many reasons, the worst of which is God's wrath. I started to get sick to my stomach. This was not what the doctor ordered. I thought that The Tower with two bodies appearing to be falling to their deaths was as bad as it looked.

The Hanged Man card didn't look much better. It has the image of a man hanging upside down, tied up by his feet. It is another of the major arcana tarot cards and one of the implications of this card basically represented the belief that a certain event or circumstance is a sacrifice that is good for you…something that in the long run, you want to have happen in your life.

Terrific. My foundations are about to collapse and I want this to happen. Right!

I now had succeeded in not only making myself more worried, but gave that worry a stronger existence in my mind. Over the course of the next two months leading up to May, I studied the cards and the book whenever I had any spare time at all. I was surprised to realize that Tarot cards do cover most of life's emotions, joys, fears, loves, sorrows…any and all events from birth to death. It is an honest and, for me at that time, an amazingly accurate reflection of events circling through life, and the power of "the Cards" began to show up in readings I would give myself.

The other effect all this had was to make me worry about my sons more than I had ever done before. I drove more carefully during this time than ever. I said no to them whenever they wanted to wander too far from home with friends. I spent two months almost never letting them out of my sight except for sending them to school. I don't think they noticed much. I let them have their friends over or came up with some idea for them to do that they liked as well, if not better. I never said anything to my husband or the boys about the fears in my head, but I made sure to do everything in my limited power to keep them around me, safe and sound. In the end, my crumbling tower had nothing to do with my sons and everything to do with my son.

The month of April came with blustery days and warming winds. In the middle of the month, my husband and I traveled with our boys to Louisville, Kentucky to visit with my brother John and his family. He had been out of the hospital for several weeks. His bones were mending, albeit slowly. The nurses, doctors, and medicines that worked to heal him were the reasons he was standing, handsome and tall. However, receiving the yellow flowers had given me some sense of belief that in our little way, my cousin Sheryl and I had been of help healing him, as well. I was beginning to understand that healing energy currents prayed for and sent flowing from the Other Side never hurt anyone. I started to believe it was possible that my thinking of yellow and the warmth of the sun had helped melt the gunk in John's lungs like warm butter. He never did get pneumonia, even after collapsed lungs, broken bones, and all the other damage to his upper body. In the big picture it was a small thing, but it did matter, if only to me.

And on a Saturday in the middle of April, my brother and I, our spouses, and all the kids went to sit along the banks of the Ohio River for the day, have a picnic, and wait for a big event called *Thunder Over Louisville*.

Believe it or not, and I didn't when I was first told this bit of trivia, but Louisville, Kentucky hosts not only The Kentucky Derby every year, but two to three weekends before the Derby, the city also hosts the world's largest fireworks display. It is called *Thunder Over Louisville*. It's the kick-off event to the Kentucky Derby Festival and is the world's largest display of pyrotechnics.

We had a glorious day!!!

Let me say that again…glory us…day.

The weather was perfect, the kids were great, our location at the bank of the flowing river could not have been better...the fireworks took our breath away...in a word, glorious.

We spread blankets and ate munchies. We sat around, talked, and played games, and, and, and.... There were loud speakers on top of large metal poles that were scattered all around to pipe out music and announcements. John explained to me that the music would be choreographed in time to the fireworks going off that night.

Throughout the daylight hours there was an air show taking place in the sky above us. Every half hour a different style plane or planes would fly above doing air tricks, loop de loops, and various skits in the air. The history of avionics was showcased over our heads as the day progressed. It was a magnificent day for all of us and I felt so extremely grateful.

At some point in the middle of the afternoon, I was just sitting by myself and quite frankly, I was thanking God for allowing me to share this day and all its memories with John...our families blending together in love and laughter. I had always thought that John and Jacquelyn's wedding day would be the best day I ever celebrated with them. But now, sitting along the riverbank I knew that was quite naïve of me then and was no longer true. This day, with all of us together, enjoying John's smiling face as we enjoyed *Thunder Over Louisville* was a bigger, better, brighter day than I could have dreamed...much bigger than their wedding day. And in my thoughts I said a very loud, but very humble and very happy, Thanks God! Thanks very, very much.

And then, well, you decide for yourself if you think that God said, "You're welcome."

Elvis started singing over the loudspeakers... *"Wise men say...only fools rush in, But I can't help falling in love with you...."* [2] You know that song; you can probably hum it to yourself...everyone knows at least bits and pieces of it. It is entitled "Can't Help Falling in Love" and was THE song that was sung at John and Jacquelyn's wedding in the middle of their ceremony, while all of the wedding party, myself included, stood at the altar. I remembered laughing to myself at the time of the wedding plans that they were having an Elvis song sung at all. I couldn't believe John and Jacquelyn were the Elvis type. But when Jacquelyn's sister-in-law had finished singing "Can't Help Falling in Love" during their wedding ceremony, there wasn't a dry eye—literally—and I completely understood why they had wanted it sung, and sung by her. She was like this exquisite angel with a perfect voice singing a perfect love song. I knew I would never forget that moment during their wedding because I had finally fully comprehended the beauty of the song itself...the words...while she gloriously sang, *"Wise men say only fools rush in, but I can't help falling in love with you...Like a river flows surely to the sea; Darling, so it goes. Some things are meant to be...."*

Now, a dozen years later and a few moments after thinking about that wedding day, those same words come back at me. As the tears rolled down, I remember thinking I was so glad that I had my back turned to everyone at that moment while I was sitting on a blanket looking out at the river. I just sat there not moving while my body tingled everywhere. A couple more songs are played and from behind me even John speaks up, "Jacquelyn, they are playing our wedding songs, babe, that's three of them in a row...."

I remember all this because I was about to find out just how big all of Who, What, When, Where, and Why can be. I was about to understand the power of The Music Man...the power of the Past brought to the Future...and those types of moments you don't forget.

The rest of April passed quietly with many warm smiles and memories for me. That was a good thing, for it was the calm before the storm. The month of May brought my tumbling tower, and it was a sacrifice I would make over and over again.

Trap Door to Sorrow

Ever been sad
on a glorious day?
Blue sky for miles,
no clouds in the way.

But that doesn't matter,
not in the least.
Your spirit's gone dark,
a shadowy beast.

There's reason to smile,
your blessings surround.
But that knowledge won't stop
all this mopin' around.

It all hangs to the left,
nothing goes right.
Your zin won't zen
no dog in your fight.

Many friends to help
get you out of this mood.
But you opt for solitaire
and an evening to brood.

Feeling pity for oneself
is the trap door to sorrow.
It snared you today,
walk around it tomorrow.

With time signals change.
Knowledge is grasped from nature
and evolves forward.

Chapter VI
Love Sends White... *The first week of May*

The month of May is my birth month and I love that fact. The heartbeat of the earth quickens at this time of year, for spring itself is being born. So much around me is blooming in May and I try to join right in.

For a variety of reasons it is a crazy month for me, my family, my husband, and many of my friends, and that is primarily because of birthdays. Mine is the 19th and I have either a family member or friend who has a birthday on the 1st, 2d, 5th, 15th, 18th, and the 28th. Of course, every year a Mother's Day is somewhere in there, and for a reason that seemed reasonable at the time and now can become ridiculous, I thought May would also be a good month for a wedding, so our wedding anniversary is on the 14th. May is a busy time in my home. It is like the month of December when it comes to expenses, events, and things to get done.

That year, a couple of weekends after our April day at *Thunder Over Louisville*, on the first Sunday of the month, the 2d of May 2001, my husband is in a motorcycle accident. Fortunately, he breaks his collarbone. Mind you, we are only two days into the start of the month and yes, I said fortunately.

***

Martin had gone for a ride with two of his longtime friends, Mike and Joe. May 1 is Mike's birthday. My husband has owned, driven, at times raced, and definitely enjoyed motorcycles for over 30 years, and for the last 20 he has gone riding with these guys. I wasn't the least worried when the three of them took off from our driveway that morning. Thirty minutes later the phone rang. Mike was on the other end telling me that Martin was going to be okay, but an ambulance was taking him to the hospital because he couldn't move his arm and he knew he had broken something. He had needed to brake too fast for some reason, lost control of the bike, and had gone flying over the handlebars.

I raced to the hospital. When he landed on his head, Martin's helmet had fortunately worked as it was designed to, and diverted the impact to his shoulders instead of his neck. He had broken his collarbone instead of cracking open his skull...or breaking his neck...or back, and I was tremendously grateful and relieved. He was able to come home with me early that same evening. I kept saying Thank You to the empty space around me that he wasn't seriously injured in his fall. Thank you, thank you, thank you....

I knew by the second of May that getting him healthy would be the main theme in our household for the rest of the month...for the next few months, actually. Everything else would take a back seat, if it even got to ride at all.

The next morning found me getting the boys off to school and making sure Martin had whatever he needed to be as comfortable as he could be. What he thought he needed was for me to go into his office and pick up his inbox work along with his briefcase and other selected items so that he could get some work done later that day. I just looked at him laying in bed and said, "Yes, dear." In my head I knew there was no way he was going to be getting any work done that day, but he would go back to sleep while I was gone to get his "work" and that was good. He would have all the info and phone numbers he needed if later in the week he actually had the energy and ability to start to get some business taken care of.

On my drive to his office, I took a few moments to say hello and thank again what I had started to feel were my "spirit friends." I was beginning to accept that many "things" surround *all of us* in the Unseen. I was slowly getting comfortable with the fact that information seemed to be passed on to me. If Martin's accident was my foundation being rocked, I could handle it quite well, especially with Their help.

In my head I found myself asking the Other Side, Okay, you have given me some indications that I am supposed to start healing and helping people through that healing. I know my own husband should be at the top of that list...but if I put my hands out over him and tell him that I am going to work with the Unseen energy around us to try to help heal his bones...Well, you all know what he will do: He is going to just laugh at me...."

In my thoughts the response comes, "His laughing at you has never stopped you from anything, especially something that is truly important to you...not a good excuse."

Yeah, well, I don't even know how I would go about this. I mean I assume I would use my hands as I did with John, but surely I don't "think yellow" with a broken collar bone...do I?

"No, my dear, you think White."

White? I think White? Why white and who is this "thinking with" me right now? Who just said, "No, my dear?"

I can't explain why I felt like I had to ask that question...I just asked it.

The response in my head came. "This is Grandfather Gordon, and you think white much like the bones themselves. I want you to think white like a bright, white, starched linen shirt."

Well, that threw me. Not the part about the white, because the white of a starched linen shirt I could definitely visualize, but I was not ready for the thought to come from Grandfather Gordon. He was one of my husband's grandfathers. I had never met any of my husband's grandparents for the simple reason that they were all "dead" many years before I knew Martin. What little history I did know of this Grandfather Gordon was that he had been a minister most of his life. He had graduated with a doctorate in Theology from Yale Divinity School at the turn of the century, been a Congregationalist minister, and started his ministry after leaving Yale by traveling to and living in Red Lodge, Montana. He spread The Word on horseback to the cowboys, Indians, and pioneer settlers. Quite a history it was, but I knew just bits and pieces of it. I had no doubt that the man had been a loving, intelligent, and fascinating man of God, but except for the few times my husband's family would reminisce about him at family gatherings, I had never given much, if any, thought to him. Now, "thoughts" in my head were trying to get me to believe that he was conversing with me.

On he went. "I want you to think about you and me working together with a fine white thread, weaving Martin's bone back together where it is broken."

Okay, I thought, I will do what I can.

It was months later before I found out more about this wonderfully proud and gentle man. One fact I hadn't known at the time was that in his later life, all Reverend Gordon wore were crisply starched, white linen shirts.

I went into Martin's office and got all the stuff he thought he needed and headed back to the house. He was sound asleep when I got home and ever so quietly, I put my hands out over his collarbone and started concentrating on weaving white threads in, through, and around this area. After a few minutes he started to stir and wake up. I pulled my hands back before he ever knew I had done anything. I thought to myself, If I could just do some healing work on him when he was sleeping, then maybe I wouldn't have to explain anything to him and risk embarrassing myself...surely that would work?

A couple hours later there was a knock on our front door. A delivery guy was holding this huge wrapped bundle in a vase. The front of the card taped to the wrapping told me his office had sent over a bouquet of flowers for Martin. Well, isn't that just so nice of them, I thought. I carried this wrapped bundle up to the bedroom and placed it on the dresser. It had several layers of paper covering the flowers inside so that it took me a minute to get it unwrapped in front of Martin.

The bouquet was solid white.

No blue or pink or purple. No yellow!

There was nothing in this huge vase but pure white flowers. There were asters, snap dragons, daisies, babies breath, roses...all—God help me—white!

I sat on the edge of the bed for a long time. Finally Martin asked me if I was okay. I started to tell my husband some of what had been going on with me. "Dear, I had a conversation with your 'dead' Grandfather Gordon this morning while I was driving to your office and I need to tell you about it...."

***

May would prove to be quite a month for Martin, as well as for me.

White Night

Light white

Sight bright

Night right?

Quite.

Insight height might fright?

Excite!

Fright might height insight

Quite.

Right night!

Bright sight

White Light

Unseen yet felt
waves in the matrix compel
streams of thought forward.

Chapter VII
Sound Truth In Sight...*The second week of May*

I was quite relieved that Martin's accident had come and gone so early in the month and the worst had happened, or so I hoped. If a motorcycle crash with a broken collarbone was my collapsing foundation, then things were going to be just fine in my life—Oh, yes Sirreey, Bob...just fine. Yet there was still something that troubled me. I was having a hard time trusting the belief that I could "hear dead people." To believe that my dear departed Great Aunt Lucille or one of my husband's grandparents was conversing with me was still just tooooo weird to truly believe, much less trust.

Between that October day traveling to my grandmother's, being serenaded on the radio, and the May morning having a bouquet of white delivered to the house, I was honestly concerned that I was losing my grip on reality. God using Elvis to sing to me on the banks of the Ohio River—as if Elvis has NOT left the building—that's CRAZY!!! Isn't it? I had reason to be concerned, for in truth, I was losing my "mind." This is a journey of the caterpillar losing its mind to gain the butterfly's soul.

By the end of the second week in May, I would buy Martin a gift that would in fact give me not only a trust in myself and what was happening around me, but a profound knowing that we are *all* spoken to by the Unseen, and that includes being spoken to by those we love that have "died"...and "spoken to" daily, if you like. I was to find out that that was, is, and always will be true, and I will be eternally grateful to the man who helped prove this to me. That his first name is a homonym for kneel doesn't surprise me at all. I have not met him so far in this life, but I will. It is only a matter of time.

The dialogue and communications between the "Other Side" and me, via the waves broadcast over the radio, hadn't stopped the day after the UK v. LSU game. It intensified. Slowly at first, but gradually the pace picked up. By the end of the second week in May, some of what was going on around me was to be explained in a manner that would take my breath away. By the end of the month, the foundations I had built my world upon were going to come tumbling down, and it was one of the most incredible things to ever happen to me.

In this chapter I need to introduce you to the Music Man and why He *was* waltzing away with my mind. Actually, the Music Man helped me realize it is not so much losing your mind as it is learning to ignore what your mind is telling you, for you cannot honestly come to know that you are talking to the Unseen around you, and more important, that the Unseen is talking back to you, unless you get "out of your mind." Your mind will tell you that you are crazy to even consider the idea that you can "hear" those who are invisible around you. It isn't possible; your mind says it sees no one there. Empty space is ALL that surrounds you. But your soul and your body tell you quite a different thing. They are supposed to. I didn't realize that then. I do now.

I have to digress a bit in my story. I am sorry for any confusion this causes, but it would have been a great deal more confusing to you if I had kept putting in bits and pieces throughout this book about the running dialogue that was going on between me and the "random" noises, phrases, songs, etc. in the world. That is not something I can explain in scattered paragraphs tucked here and there into this book. So right now I need to backtrack a little.

***

Two days after the UK and LSU football game was broadcast over my radio on the way back from visiting my grandmother, I challenged the "empty space" around me, in general, and Gary, in particular. I threw down my gauntlet...again. I had traveled to South Bend on a Saturday in October and it was now Monday morning. Martin had left for work and the boys had caught their buses to school. I made myself a cup of coffee and couldn't get the "road" trip and everything that had happened off my mind. I walked up to our stereo and out loud—to the empty space around me—I said, "Gary, if you really did what you did this weekend with the radio in my car, then right now, when I turn on this stereo you will do it again!" and I flipped the power switch to On. I had no idea whether the set up on our stereo that morning was for playing a CD or for a radio station, and I didn't check before I hit the power button. I didn't care. What happened Saturday driving to and from South Bend, if it wasn't a fluke, then it could...should...would happen again, regardless. And for me to even try to accept what had occurred in my car, it had to happen again. If not, I was going to move on down the road and not even try to attempt to figure it all out. I would act and learn to believe it didn't, hadn't, couldn't have happened.

Our stereo read "tuner" when I turned the power on, so it would be a radio station that came on and I didn't have a clue as to which station it would be, nor as I said, did I care. For a second that held my heart from beating, there was complete silence...silence on a radio station?...But before I could change the station the first notes of a song began...strings from violins played as the perfect hum of a note was sung by a woman I have always believed had the voice of an angel. I am not alone in that opinion. The beats of the tune were sounded in the waves sent through the radio...Oh, my God, I know this one...and the words were sung..."*I can read your mind and I know your story. I see what you're going*

74

through... It's an uphill climb and I'm feeling sorry, but I know it will come to you. Don't surrender 'cause you can win in this thing called love. When you want it the most there's no easy way out. When you're ready to go and your heart's left in doubt, don't give up on your faith. Love comes to those who believe it and that's the way it is....

"Don't give up on your faith. Love comes to those that believe it and that's the way it is...".[1]

The song is entitled "That's the Way It Is" and is exquisitely, beautifully, and for me in that moment, unforgettably, sung by Celine Dion. I sat down on the floor with the first words of this song coming across the radio and I hadn't moved. The last stanza being repeated over and over seemed to echo, not only at the end of the song, but deep down, in, around, and all the way through me. More tears streamed down my cheeks. The crying was becoming ridiculous and I got myself up and turned off the radio. "Well, Gary, I guess you showed me."

A couple of weeks before this, I had purchased my first Celine Dion CD. I had done it because of another song of hers that made me think of Gary every time I heard it. A year before Gary had died, in the fall of '98, Martin, Paul, Marianne, Gary, Joy, and I had gone on a house boating trip for a long weekend. Another couple, Fred and Kate, also joined us. Eight adults, four couples, away together for a few days of freedom, fun, and as much laughter as we could pack into a boat. It was to be the last long weekend we all shared together. Of course we didn't know that at the time. Those memories became so very cherished by all of us later.

We had rented a large houseboat on a lake in Kentucky and floated around together on a Friday, Saturday, and Sunday during what turned out to be a glorious Indian summer weekend in October. On that Saturday night, Gary, Joy, Paul, Marianne, Fred, and Kate decided it was a good night to watch a movie that someone had brought along. This had kind of ticked me off at the time because I wanted us to just sit and enjoy each other's company...talk, laugh, play cards, whatever. I didn't relish the idea of sitting down together on such a beautiful night and stare at a TV screen, watching a long movie. The selection of the movie also annoyed me. It was an extremely popular movie at the time, but I have never been one who enjoyed movies that seemed to entertain you using the tragedy of others. The irony that we were on a boat was not lost on me either. The movie was *Titanic*.

On Saturday night we had tied the boat off along the shore of the lake. Martin and I lit a fire and sat on the shore looking up at the stars and talking, while the others watched the movie. There must have been a meteor shower that night; Martin and I quit counting shooting stars when we reached 15. I couldn't help but hear the music of the film—the songs being sung while sitting on the shore. I certainly didn't realize at the time what that night would mean to me two years later.

The theme song for the movie *Titanic* is a magnificently written and beautifully crafted song. It is entitled "My Heart Will Go On"[2] and is exquisitely sung by Celine Dion. The movie won the Academy Award for Best Picture and this song won the Academy Award for Best Song. Though I wasn't thrilled with the main theme of the movie, the words and Celine's performance of that song had deeply touched me then.

Before Gary died, whenever I heard that song, it always brought me back to that night on the boat and all the great memories of our weekend together. That song was played a lot after the *Titanic* movie. It became one of those songs you hear replayed in all kinds of venues, from an elevator ride to being a standard song played by soft rock radio stations, ad naseum, everywhere. Two years later I would find myself buying a Celine Dion CD because of our boat trip and the song, "My Heart Will Go On," in particular. I now owned one of her CDs that was a collection of some of her greatest hits. I had purchased her CD entitled "All The Way...A Decade of Song" because the song "My Heart Will Go On" was on this CD. I had listened to the song a few times, but not too often because it always made me cry. However, I had to buy it even knowing it would do that...it's a female thing.

Now, two years later, after my own dare to the Other Side, or to Gary, or whatever, a song by Celine, with words that were so exquisitely, painfully in tune to what I was thinking and doing... *"I can read your mind and I know your story...Don't give up on your faith. Love comes to those that believe it and that's the way it is...."* That is what comes over the radio after my own dare and I started searching for the CD. I didn't have to search long because that particular CD was on top of one of the stacks of CDs sitting next to our stereo system...imagine that.

I picked up the CD case and scanned the listing of songs on the back. Well, of course it is there, I said to myself when I saw the song, "That's The Way It Is," listed on the back. I put the CD into our stereo and for the first time listened to the entire CD and spent the next hour or so listening to an earth angel sing words of love.

***

A couple of days later I was shopping at a mall for a girlfriend's birthday gift. I had admired a pair of earrings on another friend a couple of weeks before and she had told me where she had gotten them. That particular store is a franchised boutique and there is only one of them where I live. It was located in the same mall I was shopping in and when I walked by the shop I went in. I looked around and there really was nothing that day that I thought would work as a birthday gift for my friend, but they did have some beautiful earrings. One set in particular caught my eye and I asked the clerk if I could look at them because they were in a case that only salespeople could reach into. I loved them. They were teardrop-shaped little crystals hanging from tiny gold chains and glittered so magically. I looked at the price tag and went "oops," not today, out of my budget. The price was only $25 dollars, but money was very tight for me that week and I had a gift for someone to buy and it was more than I could consider spending on a pair of earrings.

In my head the thought comes, "Yes, you will buy those, too...."

Who is this...Gary?

"Yeeeessss...."

No, Gary, I said inside my head. Honey, I just don't have the money.

"Annie, the check you were expecting next week is coming in tomorrow's mail. Those earrings are perfect for you and you will buy them!"

You know how sounds can be going on around you but you don't notice, and then something in those sounds does get your attention and you notice there are sounds going on around you? Convoluted question I know, but I believe you understand what I am saying because it happens to everyone.

Muzak was playing in this little boutique. Nothing unusual, Muzak is played in most stores anymore...even the Wal-Marts of the world play something regularly in the background. Muzak is played so often that most of us ignore it, if we even notice songs are played in the first place. One song, I couldn't tell you what, had finished playing in the boutique and the first three notes were played from a flute as the next song starts and I can "name this song" in three notes. Then the words came... *"Every night in my dreams, I see you, I feel you. That is how I know you go on. Far across the distance and spaces between us you have come to show you go on...Near, far, wherever you are I believe that the heart does go on. Once more you open the door and you're here in my heart and my heart will go on and on....* "[3]

Celine was singing the theme song from *Titanic*, "My Heart Will Go On."

"Miss," I said, "I would like to buy these earrings, please."

The check paying a client's invoice on a graphic job I had completed, that I hadn't expected to receive for another week, was in my mailbox the next day.

***

It didn't seem to make a difference where I was: my car; my home; out shopping in the world; an elevator in an office building, for goodness sake; or actually in a Wal-Mart picking up cat litter. A conversation was started by the Other Side the day of the UK v. LSU game using audio waves of sound and it didn't matter where I was, the conversations continued.

A few weeks after the birthday/earring shopping trip, I was starting to get really scared. I knew that if I looked up the symptoms of schizophrenia in a medical journal, I would certainly read that believing that sounds around you were speaking to you would have to be listed in the first few sentences. I graduated from the University of Kentucky with a degree in psychology. I had studied many different psychoses getting that degree. I felt I had justification to be worried. Was I developing some mental psychosis in my middle years? That thought can send you into some terrifying scenarios.

Something else, as well, was troubling me. Gary had hardly ever gone to church, any church as far as I knew, the entire time we were friends. He would go to weddings and funerals, but I would never have referred to him as a "religious" man or very deep spiritually. A wonderful guy?

Yeah, definitely! A good friend and brother, someone to be trusted and who did nice things for others? Most assuredly. But no one would have said he was a deeply committed man of God. So how could he possibly be capable of "sending" me such strong signals when I wasn't even sure he had believed a heaven existed? I mean, surely one would have to have a very strong faith *here* to have the power *there* to send such strong messages back across. Wouldn't they?

These questions were going to lead me to the Music Man and to the realization that more was going on, much more than two old friends enjoying each other's friendship, even after the death of one of them.

***

One morning, not long after these thoughts started pestering me, I was sitting in my studio working on a graphic design project. I was looking through my stock photo collection to see if I had an image that would work for this particular project. As I flipped through the images, a picture of a pool game came flashing up on my computer screen, which of course got me thinking about my "winning" a pool tournament and Gary, and right after that a song started on the radio. It was Celine again, singing "That's The Way It Is." *"Don't give up on your faith. Love comes to those that believe it and that's the way it is."*[4] The tears started streaming…yet ridiculously AGAIN and I got mad! I had had enough. I had a lot of work to do and was too busy for this nonsense, or so I thought, and that song had truly pushed buttons with me. So somewhere in the middle of the song, I looked up into the air above me and yelled, "It's enough!!! Gary—you need to leave me alone right now…Wait a minute…This can't be Gary. Gary didn't even belong to a church. I am going to start calling you the Music Man, if that is okay with you…whoever or whatever you are. Now go away… Capiche?!!

And the thought came into my head, "Oh, I understand perfectly. I've been waiting for you to say that. You may call me the Music Man anytime you wish. Listen Up." The next song started right "up" on the radio… *"Highway run into the midnight sun. Wheels go round and round…, You're on my mind…Sendin' all my love along the wire….And **lovin' a music man ain't always what it's supposed to be**. Oh girl, you stand by me. I'm forever yours—faithfully…."*[5]

This song is sung by a group lovingly known as Journey and is called "Faithfully." It was written by J. Cain and first found on the Journey album entitled "Frontiers."

It was after this particular afternoon's musical conversation that I started conversing in my own mind with the Music Man. All music in general became a major element in my life. I had always enjoyed music being played, but a passion for music or for songs that I heard, I simply didn't possess. I did now. The radio was turned on every morning as I started work. I started to pay attention to sounds around me wherever I went. Something was said, a question answered, a new way of looking at a problem was suggested *every day* using the sounds around me. I listened to songs for the first time that I had heard for years and years. But it was different now; I was truly *listening* to the words, what was actually being said in them (to me?) and not just generically enjoying them. Was I going nuts? I kept asking myself that, over and over and over…and that in itself was driving me crazy.

One night in February, after the October drive to my grandmother's and a month before Tarot cards were to warn me of crumbling towers, I was alone folding clothes, listening to a jazz station on the radio. My husband was out of town at a meeting and I had gotten the boys to bed. A thought comes into my mind, "Ann, please turn on the TV."

I was kind of taken aback by that idea and said in my head, Why should I turn on the TV when I am listening to music?

The response comes, "Well, because I am on TV right now."

And I thought, Oh no….no, no…how in the world could You be on TV?…You have just now gotten me a little used to the idea that somehow you reach me with the radio…I am not going to allow myself to think that it also happens with the TV…that truly is madness!

And the response comes, "Annie, try not to be so melodramatic and just turn on your TV."

I got myself up and turned on the TV. It was a movie I recognized at once but had never seen all the way through. I had just watched bits and pieces of it while growing up. I had turned it on in time to see a little boy my generation had known as Opie Taylor. It was Ron Howard as a boy singing… *"Gary, Indiana; Gary, Indiana; Gary, Indiana…."*

The movie is called *The Music Man*.

***

Another morning I was walking into a Wal-Mart to pick up kitty litter and do some other shopping. There had just been a beautiful love song played on my radio and "thoughts" in my head said that had been for me…to thank me for all that I did for my kids…or so I had been told…and I was thinking in my mind, actually asking, Why are you sending me these songs, these messages so often? And as I am thinking this I just happen to walk by one of the televisions Wal-Mart has hanging from the ceiling showing different advertisements.

Without missing a beat the words come out of the TV screen, "…because I only want the best for my children…" as I walk by. It was *just* a phrase from an advertisement playing on the screen trying to sell some type of new cold remedy for kids…wasn't it?

I will never forget the afternoon I was driving along headed to the grocery store and it had been about a year since I had gotten the yellow flowers after John's accident. I was still thinking about getting a bouquet of solid yellow… "Listen up, the next song is for you," comes into my head. I can still remember what section of the road I was driving on when I first heard the name of this group and a song entitled "Yellow." The DJ piped up, as a commercial had just ended. "Here's a group to listen for in the future, called Coldplay. This is their song, 'Yellow',"[6] and out it came over my radio for the first time….

"Look at the stars, look how they shine for you and everything that you do…yeah, they were all yellow. I came along and wrote a song for you and all the things that you do and it was called yellow …I jumped across, I jumped across for you, oh, what a thing to do…for you were all yellow. I drew a line, I drew a line for you, oh, what a thing to do…you were all yellow…for you I bleed myself dry…."

It went on and on and on like that. Do I **know** that Coldplay's song "Yellow" was written for another reason besides me…many other reasons beside me? **Yes!** Do any of those band members know me in any way? No. Can I still be one of the reasons that song was written? What do you think? Could you be one of the reasons the song "Yellow" was written, or many other songs, for that matter? I know so….

Looking back, I realize the "Music Man" is around *all of us*, whether we "know" it or not. We all get stanzas of His messages now and then. My grandfather, "Pop," died in June of '99, five months before Gary died. I was with him the last day of his life. My friend Cherrie had driven me up to South Bend to visit with him and the other family members who were there with him in the hospice. Cherrie had not wanted me to drive by myself because we both knew this was the last time I would see my grandfather and it would be a hard and long trip home for me at night. I will be forever thankful to her for driving me and sharing that remarkable day with me. The day is certainly worthy of remark. My Pop was ready to cross over and showed all of us how to "face" death head on...with deep love and a glorious smile!

I had met Cherrie around 8:00 that morning at the parking lot of her church and left my car there. It was 10:00 or so that night when we got back to the lot. She dropped me off and I got into my car. I started the engine and the radio was on. A song started as I was putting on my seat belt. It was the very first time I heard a song named "Angel" masterfully sung by Sarah McLachlan.

I could go on *ad nauseam* for pages here about radio and television "coincidences" that occurred with me, but why? I believe you can start to see my point. There was a running dialogue that was going on between the Unseen and me, which I was beginning to fully understand meant *everything unseen*—the All around me. Questions were answered; a new perspective pointed out; Love sent in Waves. It was very much like the poem I wrote at the end of Chapter 3. The first time it happened I was amazed (a mazed). I felt like I had been dropped into a maze and had to find my way out. Then, the second time it happened, I felt kind of dazed. The eighth time it happened—a mind gone crazed? By the tenth time it had happened, I mean, let's face it—there wasn't much left for me to do but to the Heavens gaze.

On a fall day I am "led to believe" that I have gone on a "road trip" with Gary. That left me with a great deal to think about. That winter John has a serious car accident and yellow flowers are presented. In February I find myself communicating with a Music Man. March brings a warning from Tarot cards, what I feared to be my Ides *from* March.

April comes and Elvis is alive and well and still in the building...or at least he and the Music Man are along the banks of the Ohio River. My working with Susan and Mike and learning about "Spirit Guides" that are there for you whenever you need them, led me to think that I happened to have a spirit guide that I called the Music Man because he was really into the music scene. Did I tell anyone about the Music Man? Of course not, that is crazy talk. Isn't it?

My mind went in circles like that... truth... crazy... truth?...crazy!

I did start accepting the Truth around the pool games and the yellow flowers. Those events had started to seem down right rational to me, now that I was beginning to think I was getting advice from "dead" folks and a "spirit" I had named Music Man as they *conversed* with me over the broadcasted media waves of the world.

***

Now, fast forward to the second week in May 2001, a few weeks after the April fireworks on the banks of the Ohio River and I had the "crazy" idea that I was being communicated with via the radio and TV and a huge bouquet of white had been delivered to the house. My wedding anniversary was a few days away. Our thirteenth anniversary was on the 14th of May and quickly approaching. I didn't have a clue as to what to give my husband as a gift.

Doctors can't put a cast on anyone with a broken collar bone, so it can be slow going for the first few weeks and Martin was still very much recuperating. I certainly couldn't plan a big night out and I didn't have a clue as to what to get him for a gift. What to do? I knew he was hoping that we would just skip the whole thing, but surely I could think of something to give him that would cheer us both up.

I received an idea from Martin's Grandfather Gordon. Now, mind you, by this time I was beginning to believe that this wonderful gentleman had in some way influenced the creative juices in a florist to put together a bouquet of solid white that was destined for our home. I felt as if Martin and I had personally been given white flowers from his "dear departed" grandfather. Martin wasn't about to believe that, but that didn't really matter at that time. What mattered next was what I believed.

Grandfather Gordon, in my thoughts, suggested to me that I go to New Age People to find a gift for Martin. This was the store I had been in when I was given a Tarot card reading by Kevin and received the second opinion about falling towers. I didn't think that was a great place to find an anniversary gift for my husband, but I was certainly willing to go into the store and look around. This grandfather had in some way sent us white flowers and that was good enough for me to at least try his suggestion. So into New Age People I walked.

My friends Susan and Mike had given everyone in their "spirit classes" a reading list of books to get and I knew this store would have most of the titles that they had put on that list. One title they both had mentioned over and over as a particularly good book to help you connect with your Spirits and Angels is called *Divine Guidance* by Doreen Virtue; if nothing else, I thought this would be a good time to search for it.

New Age People is a store of candles and crystals, music and books, mystical stones and Tarot cards, fine jewelry, incense and oils. I decided as I walked through the shop that this actually might have been a good idea. I could get Martin some massage oils. Ask any husband if they would mind having a good massage given to them by their wife as part of an anniversary gift, even if they were mending from a broken collarbone. You can guess what most of them will answer, can't you? But in my thoughts, I kept hearing Grandfather Gordon saying, "No, that's not it…that's not what I had in 'mind'."

Well, I was running out of time. I had boys getting home from school soon and my husband needed checking on, so I needed to make sure this wasn't a very long shopping trip. I had my arms full of a couple of new candles and some oils and started looking through the books for *Divine Guidance.*

At the time I could have just asked a sales person to help direct me to the book, but they were all very busy. So I started looking for it myself. I knew the last name was Virtue...what a great name...easy to remember, so I figured it couldn't be that hard. But there were many sections of different books. There was a section on interpreting dreams, another on Native American spiritualism, one on Divination...it seemed to go on and on and I wasn't sure what category *Divine Guidance* would be found under. At one point I found myself putting my pile of stuff down and getting on my hands and knees looking at the bottom shelf of books under the heading of New Age Thought and trying to look through the last of the alphabet of authors...s...t...u...v...w....

"That's it!" I heard rather strongly in my thoughts, and I stopped for a moment.

That's what? I asked.

"That last book. That's the anniversary gift!" I heard Martin's grandfather tell me.

I looked back at the book and laughed out loud. I mean I laughed so hard that a woman standing next to me looked down to where I was kneeling and asked if they had a comedy section. "No," I said, "I just read something very funny was all, sorry."

In my head I was telling Grandfather Gordon that he was nuts. That book was in no way an appropriate gift for my husband for our anniversary. Martin didn't even think that it was in anyway possible—IN NO WAY, Ann, was it possible that his grandfather could "talk" to me or had somehow sent white flowers…that is the short version of what Martin had said.

Grandfather Gordon, in my head, asked me what I thought. I told him that he had heard me thank him over and over. I was in this store now at his suggestion.

"Then give Martin and yourself a magnificent anniversary gift and buy that book."

Oh, for Goodness sake, I said to the thoughts in my head. I don't have time for this. I need to get home. You did send flowers, I do believe that, so I will do as you ask. I grabbed the book without even looking through it. All I noticed was the title of the book and the front cover having a nice watercolor illustration on it. I went to the sales clerk by the register and purchased it along with some oil, a couple of candles, and a card. I went out to my car and put the bag that held a collection of things to be my husband's anniversary gift into the front seat.

The book I purchased? It is called *Conversations with God: an uncommon dialogue* by Neale Donald Walsch.

***

It was a crazy time in my house that second week in May. The boys were finishing another year of school. There were final projects, exams, field trips, and spring musical performances. Martin was of course still home and trying to heal and work at the same time. Did I mention that I run a business out of my home, as well? Things are busy and on many days I have to keep moving at a brisk pace. When I got back from the New Age People store, I brought the bag of anniversary gifts into the house, set the bag down in the guest bedroom to wrap later, and left the room.

A few days later on the afternoon of the 14th, I was busy trying to get my work done before the boys got home with homework and hungry stomachs. I was concentrating on a project, when I heard in my head, "It's time."

Time for what? I thought to myself. What time is it anyway? I looked at the clock. Oh, gosh, look at the time.

"That's what I said," I heard in my head, and then the voice said—"Anniversary?"

Yes, it is our anniversary...gifts...oh, gosh. I wanted to get Martin's presents wrapped before the boys got off the bus, or the two of them were going to want to know what I had gotten Daddy for our anniversary. I didn't really wish to get into that discussion with them. I wasn't sure myself how I was going to explain to Martin my thought process in giving him candles, massage oil, and a book entitled *Conversations with God* when he had a broken collar bone and would consider a conversation with God a ridiculous notion. The juxtaposition of those items—candles, massage oil, and a conversation with the Supreme Being? It all spun in my head. I would give Martin his gifts later, but that meant I had to get them wrapped and put away now. It was going to be the first night since his accident that the four of us would all be able to actually sit down together and have a meal. I was going to make a very special dinner. That was really enough of an anniversary gift for any of us, and had said as much to everybody the night before.

I gathered what I would need to wrap the gifts and I went into our guest bedroom to find all the stuff I had bought and hadn't touched since I had returned from the New Age People store. The bag with the candles, oil, and book was right where I had left it, and I took it and all my wrapping tools and got down on the floor. I grabbed the book and thought to myself that I probably should at least look it over before I wrap it up to give to my husband. What does a book entitled *Conversations with God* have to say anyway? The book is written by a man named Neale Donald Walsch...hmmmm,

nice illustration on the front (my graphic approval). I flipped
the book over to the back and read...

the dialogue begins . . .

I have heard the crying of your heart. I have
seen the searching of your soul. I know how
deeply you have desired the Truth. In pain have
you called out for it, and in joy. Unendingly
have you beseeched Me. Show Myself. *Explain*
Myself. Reveal Myself.

*I am doing so here, in terms so plain, you
cannot misunderstand. In language so simple,
you cannot be confused. In vocabulary so
common, you cannot get lost in the verbiage.*

So go ahead now. Ask Me anything. Anything.
I will contrive to bring you the answer. The
whole universe will I use to do this. So be on the
lookout; this book is far from My only tool. You
may ask a question, then *put this book down.*
But watch.

Listen.

The words to the next song you hear. The
information in the next article you read. The
story line of the next movie you watch. The
chance utterance of the next person you meet.
Or the whisper of the next river, the next
ocean, the next breeze that caresses your ear—
all these devices are *Mine*; all these avenues are
open to Me. I will speak to you if you will listen.
I will come to you if you will invite Me. I will
show you then that I have *always* been there.

All ways.[7]

The tears once again were rolling. I was on my knees on
the floor resting on the back of my legs, surrounded by
wrapping paper, tape, and scissors. The Madonna statue my
grandmother had given me was looking down at me. I had

placed it on a stand near the windows in this room because I thought it was the safest place for it, away from all the running and rushing around of my boys and all their friends.

"The words to the next song you hear...The story line of the next movie you watch...." A calmness I had not felt since standing in that humble little space at the hospital washed through me. I took a very deep breath and let the book open. I had taken to just letting any book I received, or was looking at, randomly open itself...at least the first time I picked it up. It isn't very hard to do and some very interesting things had happened as a consequence. The book *Conversations with God: an uncommon dialogue* opened to page 20 and I started to read at the very top of the page...

> ...always there have been, for I will not leave you without those who would show you, teach you, guide you, and remind you of these truths. Yet the greatest reminder is not anyone outside you, but the voice within you. This is the first tool that I use, because it is the most accessible.
>
> The voice within is the loudest voice with which I speak, because it is the closest to you. It is the voice which tells you whether everything *else* is true or false, right or wrong, good or bad as you have defined it. It is the radar that sets the course, steers the ship, guides the journey if you but let it.
>
> It is the voice which tells you right now whether the very words you are reading are words of love or words of fear. By this measure can you determine whether they are words to heed or words to ignore.[8]

I was so excited by what I read I was giddy and my thoughts were swimming in a whirlpool of that giddiness.

Oh...my...God...is this for real? I'm not going psychotic or even a little crazy? Is it possible that I am being spoken to, conversed with? The dialogue through music is real, these events are honest and true? Am I a part of a dialogue that continues inside my own head, my own "inner voice"? Can it be that there is no boundary, no limit to what could be done by the other side?...the Unseen Other Side—oh, God!

And the thought comes into my head, "Happy Anniversary, Ann."

Circle Weaver

She started at dawn,
as the birds informed one another
of their hopes for the day.
Flying from the post
to the waiting arms of the bramble bush,
then free falling to the grasses
ornamenting the walkway below.
Forming the triangle,
her trilogy of strength.
She wove her way to dead center,
creating the definition of a phrase
as the circles of her life she spun
designing one-of-a-kind art,
a summer's snowflake,
her fingerprint in space.
Line by line, tie by tie,
moment by moment,
until from the outer edges of her realm
to the sweet center she wove
the threaded rings of her universe.
All the while, she carried
an unborn generation on her back
in the sac Nature had obligingly created for her,
so as to keep her working
to the circle's inevitable end.
Days from now, hours from now,
innumerable trips around the center from now,
she would give birth to that generation,
giving her life in the process.
Revolving full circle, her life complete,
in the cycle of circle weavers.

Eternal is Life.
Ends tie into beginnings
forever circling.

Chapter VIII
Birth Brings Light... *The third week of May*

I cannot overemphasize to you how much reading *Conversations with God* meant to me. The more I read, the stronger I got. A belief in myself and a security in my own sanity returned after what seemed like a very long absence. It was okay...I was okay. The more I read Neale and God's dialogue, the calmer and yet more ecstatic I became. I had an understanding from the first few pages of this book that Neale was asking questions, but the answers in his thoughts, in this dialogue, were from someone else...Some One Else? I am sure many people start reading that book being quite sure that Neale Walsch is having a conversation with Neale Walsch. But after all that had happened with me, I realized after the first few pages that the thought process of the person asking the questions was quite different from the thought process answering those questions. I had the same separate sense of ideas, thoughts, and answers to my questions going on in my own head. Neale was asking questions to what I had referred to in my own thinking as the Other Side, the Unseen...the Music Man...and Neale was getting answers coming back as well...from the Unseen, the Others. He says he is conversing with God...was I?

***

My wedding anniversary evening with Martin and our boys came and went. We had a great dinner and later, after the kids were in bed, I gave Martin what I told him were "our" gifts. We would both enjoy all the goodies I had wrapped up. Martin thought the book had an interesting title, but he was much more enthusiastic about the candles and massage oils. Imagine that. Martin assured me he had no problem with my reading the *Conversations* book first...no surprise there either.

I began to inhale the pages. I was getting my grip back on reality and felt for the first time in a long time that everything was really going to be okay.

The third week of May arrived and with it would come a celebration for my day of birth as a butterfly. By the end of this week the caterpillar would be completely gone. I would quit struggling in my cocoon, surrender, and give Up. There would be nothing left for me to fight with. You will understand why by the end of this chapter. After you read what happens next, it may not be enough for you to quit struggling, but you will understand why I did. God, the Creator, Allah, the One, Jehovah, the Source, Infinite Intelligence, the Great Spirit, the Holy Mystery—*whatever* semantic choice you wish to make...my Creator would push me up and out of my protective cocoon to release the butterfly.

This, however, is the week I am terrified of relating to you and at the same time, most look forward to reaching, writing, and getting beyond. For me this chapter is about my struggle of Love against Fear, a Divine dichotomy, as Neale and God would point out to me. I now understand that we must have both for either to exist.

I made a difficult choice when I was young, a huge choice in anyone's life, and my decision as to what to choose was based mostly on Fear. I didn't know then what I know now. Who does?

I have been given the enormous Gift of having a very similar choice to make again. I have been led to the same ground to walk all over, albeit from another perspective, in a different time. I can again choose Fear this time and completely skip writing this chapter. Fear tells me there is no reason for anyone to know about any of this. Fear has a valid point, as it always seems to, which is what can make Fear so dangerous. But I would know that I had once again denied a deep and honest Love out of Fear. I would have once more not chosen my son out of Fear, as opposed to giving myself the opportunity to hold him tight with Love. Can *I* choose Fear again, especially when my son has made it clear to me that he has chosen me out of Love—again?

However, seeing the path that is laid before you and walking it are two very different things. Love shows us we are never walking alone on any path, but Fear leads us to believe the opposite is true because it so vividly "looks" like we are completely alone. The path of Fear will often portray itself as a much easier stroll than Love; the ease of silence alone will keep you holding Fear's hand as you walk along.

I was helped at this time because of Neale's transcribing his *Conversations with God*. In their dialogue, I was given the words of Love I was going to need to get through what was going to be given to me as my birth day gift. Neale's book gave me a wonderful question to help me find God's Truth to hold onto—in all moments, to hold onto with the knowledge that this question always produces the correct answer. I held onto it then and I do so now with a much stronger, knowing grip. The question God always would have us ask to find the correct way to go in any circumstance is *What would Love do now?*[1]

Love writes this chapter.

***

There is a time when acceptance of the change, a comfort with the transformation, begins. For the caterpillar it is the beginning of the end and the light starts to pour into the cocoon. Many times, if it hasn't already happened, this is when the question is finally asked, "Why me?" And one hopes that if there truly is a God, that God would respond by saying, "Why not you?"

But I believed there was a very big reason for God to put a big "Not You" sign around my neck. I was asking the question "Why me?" because of a very deep and high wall only God and I knew I had built over 20 years earlier; a wall of pain and fear, if you will. I could use this wall to stop my metamorphosis from going further. I could easily decide that what I had done was more than enough to stop this whole "spiritual" thing from proceeding, but I was about to find out my fears weren't going to stop the Unseen from getting a very powerful message through to me. God was not going to let my choices in life that had in my head and heart "walled me in," prevent me from continuing our Dialogue and spreading Love anywhere and everywhere I could in this life. But to do that my walls had to come tumbling down…and God is the only "One" that could do that.

Early in my life I had done what some people may consider unforgivable and condemn me. The Monsignor who had chewed me out at 13 because I was "that type" of girl might feel justified in saying, "I told you so." Because of what I had done, some of you may not be able to believe that God would forgive me, much less have a dialogue with me. That is okay…but that is not what God said to me. How does God go about forgiving the so-called unforgivable? What does God do now?

What does Love do now?

***

In April, at Susan and Mike's monthly class, I had mentioned to everyone that for my birthday in May I wanted to treat myself to a special "psychic" event of some kind. I wanted to go to a séance, or have a very experienced medium read my Tarot cards and "speak to my spirit guides." Several months before this, my cousin Sheryl had started attending these same meetings, and that night she told me that what I might consider doing is having a "card reading" done like Jennifer. She was another woman in our group and we were having this meeting at Jennifer's house. She enthusiastically agreed. "Oh, Annie," she said, "You have to see if this guy can do a reading for you and make you a card like he did for me." I asked what having a "card done" meant, and Jennifer proceeded to go get her "card" and bring it out to show everyone.

When she handed me this exquisite card she had received from this guy, I was once again a mazed. The "card" was a regular 3″ x 5″ index card. On one side was a beautiful painting, and I do mean beautiful. It looked like Monet had done a painting on an index card. Jennifer's illustration was of an exquisite white swan in the middle of a majestically painted lily pond. The swirling of color and the intricacy of detail astounded me. However, Jennifer was more excited by what was on the back of the card. As she flipped over her card, Jennifer explained that on the back was written the first *and last* names of a few of her family members who had died. There were also the names of some of her spirit guides. She went on to explain that she had never met nor seen the guy that did these cards before the night she went to his "card reading." "Annie," she said, "He never met me, he had no idea that I had a grandfather and an aunt on the other side, but he was able to write down their first *and last* names."

I was astounded and said a very big "YES, this is exactly what I would like to do, or get, or whatever, for my birthday. How do I get one of these?!?"

Susan explained that there was a guy named Joe who lived about 45 minutes northeast of us, and he had groups of people into his home and gave each person a small "reading" from the Other Side, and then he gives you a card with a picture on one side and names on the other. Each card is different. All I needed to do was to call him on the phone and set up an appointment for whichever night worked best in our schedules.

Sheryl had wanted to go see Joe as well, so she and I talked about getting her sister Emily and their mother, my Aunt Geri, to come with us. Susan told me how to get Joe's phone number to make an appointment. I was excited driving home that night from Jennifer's. I had found something to give myself for my birthday that year...a very different something... something mysterious...or at the very least, unique. Little did I know.

I called Joe a couple of days later and made an appointment to come to his house on the evening of the third Saturday in May for one of his "card" gatherings. That Saturday I met Sheryl and two other women, Molly and Sarah, at a bookstore near the expressway. We all piled into Sheryl's SUV because she had volunteered to drive us up to James' place. Molly and Sarah had both been at Jennifer's the night she had shown us all her card and they had decided to join us. My Aunt Geri and Emily had not been able to go. I had been a little disappointed, but I really enjoyed the company of these three women and we all headed to James' house very excited.

About an hour later we were standing in front of Joe's house with about ten other people. He would let us all in at 7:00 p.m. exactly. When 7:00 arrived, the front door opened and Joe came out and introduced himself. He then led us into the first room in his house. It was a fairly large room with chairs lining three walls. At one end there was a large desk and a chair facing all the other chairs. There was a very large painting of a young man on the wall behind the desk, but little else in this room.

About ten minutes after we had walked into this room, more people had arrived and all the seats were filled. There were about 16 people plus Joe. We were all sitting as he opened this gathering with a small prayer of thanks to God for the messages that were about to be sent. He then proceeded to call out someone's name. When they had responded that they were there, he started giving them messages from their loved ones and guides from the "Other Side." Joe spoke for a few minutes with each person in that room. It took about an hour and by 8:00 p.m. he had given each of us messages. He had told me that my grandmother and a friend named Gary were very close to me and were sending their love...always. He said I had a few men around me that loved me very much. I thought of my grandfathers. He said a few other things to me and then talked to my cousin Sheryl who was sitting next to me about our Grandfather, Pop, but I can't remember any of it. Something was to happen that would make most of what he said of little consequence in comparison to what he was about to give to me.

After he had spoken to everyone, he started to hand out the index cards. On the back of each card was the person's name that was attending that night. He called out your name and when you responded, he walked over and handed your card to you. I happened to be one of the last that was given a card. After Joe handed out the last card, he suggested we all stand up, walk around, and look at each other's cards.

When I had first looked at the card I had been given, I was dumbfounded. There was an incredibly detailed painting of a young man, standing on a mountainside with other mountains in the distance. There was a big brown bear in the background. A real bear just looking at me, as was this young man in a very "real" way. This young man was on a grassy hill with rocks scattered near him. He did not look scared of the bear at all. He was not really smiling big, but not frowning. He was just standing there with mountains in the background and a bear with him, as if he had some wild nature pet.

When I first looked at the picture of this young man I had thought to myself, "That looks like Dirk!" and a huge chill went up and down my spine.

After Joe handed out the rest of the cards the room got very noisy; everyone was so excited. Cards were being passed around while each of us tried to figure out what the images meant to us and comparing styles of art in the pictures. Each card was wonderfully unique. Some cards were very detailed, with intricate backgrounds, and others were simple portraits. The range in style of art on these cards seemed to go from Renoir, Monet, or Picasso to Peter Max, Andy Warhol, or a high school art student. The art on these cards were all incredibly varied in form, color, and style.

A few minutes went by and then I found myself just staring down at my card again. The eyes in this young man made me smile. His hair, his build, the way he stood...he looked so much like a young Dirk, as I had imagined Dirk to look before I had met him.

I asked in my head, Who is this, please? This looks so much like Dirk but it is not. This guy looks like he could be one of Dirk's brothers, more than Dirk's brothers looked like Dirk. But it isn't...what does this card mean? Who is this, please?

In my thoughts I heard, "Sit down, Ann."

What?...Sit down? Why do I need to sit down?...Okay, I'm sitting down...Did Dirk die?! Are you trying to tell me he is on the Other Side? But this isn't Dirk—it just looks so much like him. Now, who is this PLEASE?!

And in my head I hear, "Annie, this is a picture of your son."

***

Dirk...Dirk is the reason I met Gary, and a whole host of friends I still have. He introduced me to Mother Sarah, who was the matriarch of a group of friends I have had for a very long time. Kay, Billy, Paul and Marianne, Blackey, Joy; I could go on for a number of paragraphs here, but I won't. A group of friends I met through Dirk I am still friends with over 25 years later. Dirk is the only one none of us has seen in years. He was called Dirk because it was a family name from long ago. He left town over 20 years ago and hasn't been heard from since.

At the beginning of my junior year in college, I had taken a part time job at a small jazz club in Lexington and that is where I first met him. We started dating and became involved with each other very quickly. Dirk was 33 years old, divorced, and a father of two.

His kids were living with their mom out of state and Dirk was my mother's nightmare come true. I was all of 20. I was young, and to say I was naïve is to be kind.

He was not what you would call financially stable or in any way the type of man you take home to meet mom. But I did. Dirk was very street smart and extremely well read, but he had little, if any, ambition. He was a talented stonemason and worked hard with his hands, but irregularly. A "good catch" would not have been used to describe him. However, he was great fun to be around, extremely charismatic, and I "fell" for him. We ended up having a relationship that lasted a little over two years.

The summer at the end of my junior year we rented half of a duplex together. It was definitely NOT with my parents' blessing. But I had gotten a full time job to earn some money and stayed in Lexington to work and be with Dirk. It was during that summer that I first became friends with a wonderful group of people that he had introduced me to, and that is how I first met Joy and Gary.

It was a great summer for me. I had new friends, a new job, and I loved Dirk very much. I knew deep down that he was not the kind of guy I would spend the rest of my life with, but I was in no hurry for any commitment. I worried mostly about two things: getting through college and having fun. There is nothing in life that can create tragedy as quickly as being young, fun loving, and foolish.

In December of 1980, during my senior year in college, just over a year after Dirk and I first started dating, I found out I was pregnant.

My world seemed to come crashing down around me. I was on birth control pills at the time; I wasn't that naïve and stupid. I couldn't figure out for a long while how it ever did happen. I didn't know then that antibiotics could affect whether you were truly protected or not. I had gone to the health clinic the month before for some type of chest flu and had been put on antibiotics for a couple of weeks. The not knowing "how" it happened didn't change a thing; the damage was done, I was pregnant, and I have never been so scared...before or since.

Even now, writing all this out does not scare me as deeply as I was terrified then. And having to tell family members 20-plus years after the fact about some deep, dark secret you have kept to yourself is enough to get most people shaking in their boots. I am no exception. Today the shaking is in my boots; back then I was shaking all over. I was scared of being and staying pregnant, and I was just as scared of what I would have to do to not be pregnant.

From the moment I first realized that my menstrual cycle was "late" until many months later, when all had been said and *done,* I thought of very little else besides the fact that I was pregnant, and then that I wasn't pregnant, and everything that had happened in between. I don't believe most people understand that most women who find themselves pregnant and thinking of ending that pregnancy think of little else. Judgments are made by so many others: "If these women would only think it through...," not realizing that for most of us, little else is done but a constant thinking it through. It is a choice that goes up, down, around, and entirely "through" you. It is definitely a decision that can stay with your psyche for years, if not for the rest of your lifetime. No one goes through an ending of a pregnancy, any type of ending, without a scar of some type. Mine would become quite deep.

Dirk didn't think my "condition" was much more than that, a condition you can take care of. He had two children from his first marriage and wasn't about to have any more. To him there was only one correct choice.

I need to state, as bluntly as I can, that Dirk is *not* the bad guy here. He could have gotten on his hands and knees as soon as I told him and begged me to marry him, but I can't tell you that I would have said, "Oh, yes, Dirk, Yes!" and everything would have been hunky dory. That's not true. It scared me to think I *would* be tied to him for the rest of my life. I knew that happily ever after just wasn't possible for him and me. Marriage would solve very little and could actually make things worse *for ever after*.

I was sad and lost and didn't know where to turn. I knew at the time there were programs in place to get help. I went to Planned Parenthood, and thanked God it was there…I still very much thank God for Planned Parenthood for all the people that that organization helps in many, many ways. I talked to a wonderful woman who explained all my options. They would help me find an adoption service; they would help me find programs to continue the pregnancy. I went through the motions of listening, but deep down I knew I didn't have the courage or the heart it would take for me to have a baby. I couldn't, which in truth means wouldn't, tell my parents. I wasn't brave enough to go to them and ask them to help me take care of a baby. They still had two of my three siblings under their roof, and I never had been the type to go out of my way to trouble them financially any more than I had to. I wasn't going to start now by showing up bearing their first grandchild for them to help at least financially raise. They would have helped me any way they could. I knew that then; I know that now. They are wonderful parents. Unfortunately, I was anything but prepared to be a wonderful parent myself. Raising a child alone, or with help, was just not something I believed I could possibly do. Even if I had had the nerve to go away and carry the baby to term, only then to give it away...that hurt me to the core just thinking about it. I knew there would be no way I could feel anything grow inside me and be able to walk away from "it." I was, in my mind, trapped by circumstances and I stayed trapped out of Fear.

At the time I was mainly thinking about what was best for me. It is very hard for me to have to admit that now, but that is the simple truth. I tried to tell myself at the time that I was doing what was best for me and for everyone else involved, but the truth was I was operating entirely out of Fear: deep-seated, gut-wrenching Fear. And it was *mostly* mine.

I didn't breathe a word of this to any friends or family, no one. Sound familiar?

In January of 1981, I did what Dirk wanted and what I thought was the best thing for everyone concerned. I had an abortion.

I stayed in bed for days. Not because I had to, but because I wasn't sure how to get back up and start again. Dirk ended up telling one of our friends, Bill, about what we were going through. I realize now that he had to talk with someone, but then I was furious with Dirk. Bill said he would never tell anyone and I believed him. He never did. Bill has been a tremendous friend to me ever since. For a few years after this time, I worried someone besides Dirk or Bill would find out, but no one ever did. The only other person who ever found out was Martin, and that is because I told him. At some point before we got married, I told him about my getting pregnant when I had been with Dirk and that I had had an abortion.

Martin was very kind and loving when I told him. We talked about it 'til all his questions were answered and I had said all I needed to say. We seldom mentioned it again. I was thankful for his understanding and his silence. No one beside those three men would ever know...or so I believed.

I went into a depression right after the abortion. Many would judge and say that is the least I could do and they might be right. When I look back on it now, I think I went into a depression the day I found out that I was pregnant and stayed there for quite a while after everything had been said and "done." I stayed home for weeks just crying. I stayed away from people and gatherings. I went to work but not much else. It was definitely the beginning of the end of the relationship for Dirk and me as a couple.

I had told my parents during the Christmas break that I was going to take a semester off from school. They had no way of knowing what was really going on with me. I was only a few weeks pregnant during the holidays, so I was far from physically looking any different. They didn't like the idea of my taking a semester off because I was so close to finishing, but I explained I was burnt out and my grades reflected that. I told them that I wanted to work full time and I would go back to finish up during the summer or fall and get my degree. I did go back to classes the next fall and finished with my degree from college. I also finished up with Dirk. I moved after I graduated and left him behind, but I didn't leave the experience behind.

Every Christmas for years afterwards, I thought of the pregnancy and what I had done or what I hadn't done, depending on how you look at it. I didn't know why, but I had always felt that if I had gone ahead with the pregnancy, the baby would have been a boy. I always seemed at some point during the holidays to try to figure out how "old" my son would have been for whatever Christmas it was. I would sit and think about what I would get for a "boy" his age to put under whatever Christmas tree I found myself sitting around.

It was probably eight to ten years after that December/ January "season" before I quit being sad during some of the holidays, and even then I never forgot and always had at least a day or two of melancholy. No one knew and no one noticed. This secret and the incredibly private pain that it carries with it was going to be the same, hidden and kept to myself.

But now, now things are very different.

***

I am sitting in Joe's front room, surrounded by people all mingling about and comparing their spirit "cards." I sat looking down at this picture that had been handed to me of this handsome young man. How many years had it been?…20…He would be 20 now, just about the age I was when it all swirled in my life so long ago…just about how old this young man looks in this picture. The eyes, the warm but very intense eyes; the dark brown color and wave in the hair were indeed Dirk's, but the shape of the face, the nose and chin, that is what was different. I finally realized why the young man in this picture wasn't a mirror image of Dirk: he had some of my features, as well. This handsome face's features were a beautiful blending of Dirk and me.

Oh God, I am soooooo sorry, I screamed in my head. How is this possible? What is going on?

"That is indeed your son, Annie," I heard in my thoughts. "That is a picture of him now; his name is Jake."

Now?!? My son was never born. How is this a picture of my son now?!? I screamed to the Other Side in my head. THAT IS NOT POSSIBLE!?!

"Whether or not your son was 'born' is a matter of definition. Whatever choice anyone makes about giving birth or not giving birth does not stop what Is. You didn't 'kill' Jake, but you did stop yourself from *giving to him birth in your life*. Now let me ask you a question, Annie. Is Gary dead? Gone? Never to be 'seen' or 'heard' from again?"

No, I answered, I realize now he is gone from my "eye" sight, but he is not dead. I do hear him; we seem to be able to at times "think together."

"Wonderful! Happy Birth Day!!! Right answer; he is on one side of you right now. I am very thrilled that you KNOW that and will say it as Truth. But you must begin to realize this...make this REAL in your heart because it is also Truth. Jake is also with you, right here, right now! No one dies...ever! Not Jake, not Gary, no One!"

If there had not been 17 other people in that room, I might have had a complete emotional breakdown right then and there. As it was, I was shaking and trying very hard not to let anyone know.

What I had wished to show up on the card for my birthday was for my grandmother Ruth and Gary's full names to be on the back of the card. That was all I hoped for. I certainly hadn't given much, if any, thought as to what the picture on my card would be. All I truly wanted was for Joe, who didn't know me at all—we had never met before that night—if somehow he had been able to put Grandma and Gary's names on the back of my card...first, as well as last names! Now that would be quite a gift to me. The wish I had before I ever entered this room finally occurred to me, and after holding this card for probably 20 minutes, I remembered what I had hoped to see on the back. Shaking, already *knowing* that I would indeed have that part of my wish granted, I flipped the card over and looked. Gary's full name was indeed there, as was my grandmother's, with the added touch of having a heart over her name...a heart? After the truth of what I had done was shown in this card? A little heart drawn above my grandmother's name? How does that work? My mind was a cyclone looking for a place to land.

A few moments later, Joe opened his front door, thanked us all for coming, and we filed out. I didn't say much of anything on the drive home. I'm not sure that I could have spoken out loud, but thankfully I didn't have to. Sheryl, Molly, and Sarah were so excited by the images on their cards and the names on the back that they talked the whole way back to the bookstore's parking lot.

Sheryl picks up on things pretty well and she asked me if I was okay when we got back to my van. She had asked who the guy was on my card and I told her I was still trying to figure that out. I reassured her that I was fine, just tired. She understood; it had been a long Saturday for all of us. Sarah and Molly got in their cars and headed out of the parking lot behind Sheryl. I just sat in my car and cried my eyes out for a while.

I kept apologizing to Jake and God and the Unseen world around me. I had been saying it over and over in my mind for well over an hour now and finally I could say it out loud in the privacy of my car.

I cried it out, "I am sooooo very sorry, Jake! Oh, God, please forgive me...please...."

I kept saying it because I kept hearing everyone answer in my thoughts, "There is nothing to forgive," and I was terrified I was going crazy...again. How can anyone, especially God, say there is nothing to forgive?!?

***

The phrase "there is nothing to forgive" had been haunting me since Gary's funeral and that had been for over a year and a half at this point. At the end of Gary's "wake," I had been standing waiting to say goodnight to Joy, and deep down in my thoughts comes, "Please go up to Mark, give him a hug, send him my love and thanks for all he's done for me and all he's done for Joy." Looking back now, I realize that "thought" was the beginning of the dialogue between Gary and me.

Mark was one of Gary's good friends. He was the first person Joy had called after she had come home to find Gary still in bed and had called 911. Mark had done everything and anything Joy needed him to do as far as getting the funeral arrangements done, phone calls made. He was unconditionally there. I thought giving him a hug of thanks was a good idea and certainly couldn't hurt. So I did just that; I went up to Mark, gave him a huge hug, and whispered in his ear that Gary wanted me to tell him thanks for all he had done for Gary and all he was doing for Joy.

Mark picked me up off my feet, swirled me around, and thanked me profusely. He told me I had no idea how much my saying that meant to him.

The next day after Gary's funeral, I found out that Mark had done something to Gary that I considered very hurtful to Gary. There is no need for me to go into detail because it doesn't matter what it was, as much as it matters that I considered it wrong — a stab in a friend's back. I felt so terribly guilty about hugging Mark at the funeral and thanking him for Gary. How could I have been stupid enough to do that? I believed that Gary was the last person that would have thanked Mark. I am sorry, Gary, for saying that to him, I kept apologizing in my thoughts, as if I could honestly converse with a dead man. But what kept me continuing the conversation in my head was the "response" I kept getting back in my thoughts. I couldn't understand how I could keep answering myself in my "head" with the "thought," "Don't be sorry, Annie, there is nothing to forgive."

Now, a year and a half later, I was in possession of an incredible image on an incredible card. Could I believe once again in the incredible, non-credible circumstance I found myself in? Could I believe the "thoughts" that were swirling in my head? How is it possible for anyone in this situation to say to me, much less believe, "there was nothing to forgive" about what I had done?

That simple and powerfully complex phrase had circled back around in my life and I wasn't any closer to understanding it now than I was after Gary's funeral. If anything, I was more confused. I could now accept that Gary could tell me there was "nothing to forgive" when it came to Mark's disloyal behavior. In comparison to what I had done and been confronted with, Mark's behavior was as if he had done no more than not paying back a $20 Gary had loaned him to buy beer; that is forgivable. What I had done is not…can't be…can it?

***

I drove home from the bookstore's parking lot that night with the radio and any other form of audio turned OFF. I couldn't handle any more at that point.

Martin had stayed up waiting for me to get home from my "card reading." I had hoped he was going to already be in bed when I got home because I wasn't sure if I would be able to vocalize to him what had happened without totally losing control. But he was up, sitting on the couch reading. He looked at me and got a concerned look on his face as he asked if I was all right and how the evening had gone. I just kind of handed him the card and sat there. He looked at it for a few minutes, turned it over, and saw Gary and my grandmother's names on it and just looked at me. Slowly, one word at a time, I told him what had happened and what had been told to me in my "thoughts." Martin had a surprise for me, as well. He had seen maybe one or two photos of Dirk, somewhere along the way. When Martin first looked at the picture on the card, even *he* had thought of Dirk.

Needless to say, I didn't sleep much that night. The next day was Sunday and it started out very dark and gray, like my thoughts. Of course, I woke up thinking about what all had happened the night before. A picture of a young man...my son?...is it possible?...named Jake....

I made the three males in my house a big breakfast. I was bound and determined to spoil them that day...all three of them. I was consciously trying to make up for what I had done to one son...one son?...I was completely aware that I was trying to somehow appease my own conscience. I fixed all their favorite breakfast goodies. After the dishes were cleaned up, I looked around and everyone was gone. My boys had gone to play with the neighbor boys down the street and my husband had started the lawn mower.

Now, after years of suppressing any thoughts at all about my unwanted pregnancy and what I had done, I had been given an unmistakable, unequivocal reminder as my birthday gift.

"Oh, God, I am soooooo very sorry...." I could the feel the tears coming again and these to me were in no way ridiculous.

"Annie, my dear, please stop," comes into my thoughts. "Go get your books, all three of them, and go sit outside. Get some fresh air, it will help clear your head and your heart. You will feel much better. I promise."

Shortly after I had started reading *Conversations with God,* I had realized that it was the first book in a three-part trilogy. Neale Donald Walsch had transcribed more *Conversations with God* and there was a *Book 2* and a *Book 3*. I had already gone to a bookstore to get them because I knew that I would want to read them as soon as I finished Book I and I was almost done.

I grabbed all three books. It was a good idea. I could sit in the warmth of the day as I finished reading *Book 1*. The books are written in a type of question and answer format.

Neale asks a question or makes a comment and then it is God's turn. It is a running dialogue — one of the most powerful I have ever been privy to.

I set the pile of books down onto our picnic table and sat down. I heard, "Take the book on top and just let it open...as you like to do."

Book III was on top of the pile and I picked it up and let it open.

It opened onto page 246, and a thought comes, "2...4...6...8...Who do we appreciate?"

Very funny, I thought, I am in deep pain here, God, and you make jokes?

"And if I can't make jokes with you when you are in deep pain, especially when you think that deep pain has to do with disappointing Me, then who can?"

And I began to read. The top of the page begins with a statement from God:

> That's a great metaphor. That's how it is with souls. The One Soul—which is really All There Is—reforms Itself into smaller and smaller parts of Itself. All the "parts" were there at the beginning. There are no "new" parts, merely portions of the All That Always Was, reforming Itself in what "looks like" new and different parts.[9]

And then a comment from Neale:

> **There's a brilliant pop song written and performed by Joan Osborne that asks, "What if God was one of us? Just a slob like one of us?" I'm going to have to ask her to change the lyric line to: "What if God was one of us? Just a glob like one of us?"**

Ha! That's very good. And you know, her song *was* a brilliant song. It pushed people's buttons all over the place. People couldn't stand the thought that I am no better than one of them.

That reaction is an interesting comment, not so much on God, but on the human race. If we consider it a blasphemy for God to be compared to one of us, what does that say about us?

What, indeed?

Yet You *are* "one of us." That's exactly what You're saying here. So Joan was right.

She certainly was. Profoundly right.

I want to get back to my question. Can You tell us anything about when life as we know it starts? At what point does the soul enter the body?

The soul doesn't enter the body. The body is enveloped by the soul. Remember what I said before? The body does not house the soul. It is the other way around.

Everything is always alive. There is no such thing as "dead." There is no such state of being.

That Which Is Always Alive simply shapes itself into a new form—a new physical form. That form is charged with living energy, the energy of life, always.

Life—if you are calling life the energy that I Am—is always there. It is never *not* there. Life never *ends*, so how can there be a point when life *begins*?

C'mon, help me out here. You know what I'm trying to get at.

Yes, I do. You want Me to enter the abortion debate.

Yes, I do! I admit it! I mean, I've got God here, and I have a chance to ask the monumental question. When does life begin?

And the answer is so monumental, you can't hear it.

Try me again.

It *never* begins. Life *never* "begins," because life never *ends*. You want to get into biological technicalities so that you can make up a "rule" based on what you want to call "God's law" about how people should behave—then punish them if they do not behave that way.

What's wrong with that? That would allow us to kill doctors in the parking lots of clinics with impunity.

Yes, I understand. You have used Me, and what *you* have declared to be *My laws*, as justification for all sorts of things through the years.

Oh, come on! Why won't You just say that terminating a pregnancy is murder!

You cannot kill anyone or anything.

No. But you can end its "individuation"! And in our language, that's *killing*.

You cannot stop the process wherein which a part of Me individually expresses in a certain way without the part of Me that is expressing in that way agreeing.

What? What are You saying?

I am saying that nothing happens against the will of God.

Life, and all that is occurring, is an expression of God's will—read that, *your will*—made manifest.

I have said in this dialogue, your will is My will. That is because there is only One of Us.

Life is God's will, *expressing perfectly*. If something was happening *against* God's will, it couldn't happen. By definition of Who and What God Is, it *couldn't happen.* Do you believe that one soul can somehow *decide something* for another? Do you believe that, as individuals, you can affect each other in ways in which the other does not want to be affected? Such a belief would have to be based on the idea that you are separate from each other.

Do you believe that you can somehow affect life in a way in which God does not want life to be affected? Such a belief would have to be based on an idea that you are separate from Me.

Both ideas are false.

It is arrogant beyond measure for you to believe that you can affect the universe in a way with which the universe does not agree.

You are dealing with mighty forces here, and some of you believe that you are mightier than the mightiest force. Yet you are not. Nor are you *less* mighty than the mightiest force.

You *are* the mightiest force. No more, no less. So let the force be with you!

Are You saying that I can't kill anybody without his or her permission? Are You telling me that, at some higher level, everyone who has ever been killed has *agreed* to be killed?

You are looking at things in earthly terms and thinking of things in earthly terms, and none of this is going to make sense to you.

I can't *help* thinking in "earthly terms." I am *here*, right *now*, on the Earth!

I tell you this: You are "in this world, but not of it."

So my earthly reality is not reality at all?

Did you really think it was?

I don't know.

You've never thought, "There's something larger going on here"?

Well, yes, sure I have.

Well *this is what's going on. I'm explaining it to you.*

Okay. I got it. So I guess I can just go out now and kill anybody, because I couldn't have done it anyway if they hadn't agreed!

In fact, the human race acts that way. It's interesting that you're having such a hard time with this, yet you're going around acting as if it were true anyway.
Or, worse yet, you are killing people *against* their will, as if it didn't matter!

Well, of *course* it matters! It's just that what we want matters *more*. Don't You get it? In the moment we humans kill somebody, we are not saying that the fact that we've done that doesn't matter. Why, it would be flippant to think that. It's just that what *we* want matters *more*.

I see. So it's easier for you to accept that it's okay to kill others *against* their will. This you can do with impunity. It's doing it because *it is* their will that you feel is wrong.

I never said that. That's not how humans think.

It isn't? Let Me show you how hypocritical some of you are. You say it is okay to kill somebody *against* their will so long as *you* have a good and sufficient *reason* for wanting them dead, as in war, for instance, or an execution—or a doctor in the parking lot of an abortion clinic. Yet if the other person feels *they* have a good and sufficient reason for wanting *themselves* dead, you may not help them die. That would be "assisted suicide," and that would be wrong!

You are making mock of me.

No, *you* are making mock of *Me*. You are saying that I would *condone* your killing someone *against* his will, and that I would *condemn* your killing someone in *accordance* with his will.
This is insane.
Still, you not only fail to see the insanity, you actually claim that those who *point out the insanity* are the ones who are crazy. *You* are the ones who have your head on straight, and they are just troublemakers.
And this is the kind of tortured logic with which you construct *entire lives* and *complete theologies*.

I've never looked at it quite that way.

119

I tell you this: The time has come for you to look at things in a new way. This is the moment of your rebirth, as an individual and as a society. You must re-create your world now, before you destroy it with your insanities.

Now *listen to Me*.

We are All One.

There is only One of Us.

You are not separate from Me, and you are not separate from each other.

Everything We are doing, We are doing in concert with each other. Our reality is a co-created reality. If you terminate a pregnancy, We terminate a pregnancy. Your will is My will.[9]

The Blueprints of God

Pay heed to coincidence, for Life's game is at play.
Nothing "just" happens in a haphazard way.
Events are not random that make up a day.

We've all had the moments pieces fall into place.
Circumstances are perfect: the right time, the right space.
A brutal tragedy's defeated...by a saving grace.

A book falls opens to the needed page.
Opportunity knocks as if cued to the stage.
Perfect music is scored, defining an age.

Then a heart's torn to pieces from immeasurable grief,
the wrong place, the wrong time, with no sign of relief,
leaving the devout even questioning belief.

There at a sign is perceived, a message comes through.
A Spirited Hello, with much love sent to you.
One heals with the salve of knowing what's true.

"Timing is everything" isn't uttered by nuts.
The chance in encounters is anything but.
Fortune's luck of the draw begins with the cut.

I don't mean to suggest that we don't have a choice,
options to opt from, an opinion to voice.
The freedom to hate or in love to rejoice.

You create your destiny one day at a time.
You may do it with reason, you can do it with rhyme,
as lousy stuff happens when life turns on a dime.

But in Always there's purpose to this grand façade.
Fate has built empires, history changed with a nod;
a design to the universe, the Blueprints of God.

Two events coincide to give you a clue.
Especially when dropped right out of the blue.
Heaven sent direction, a suggestion or two.

The Plan's so much grander than most mortals believe.
You may harvest serendipity but God plants the seed,
with the love and the knowledge that what will be will be.

Kisses like tears flow
out of intimate senses.
Release deep waters.

Chapter IX
Dream Lake

Can I honestly think that a Jake exists?

Right now you may believe I need that intense psychological counseling I mentioned earlier. You may begin to worry that you do, as well, because you are starting to believe me. As you are reading these words you might find it easier to believe I am from another planet and several government agencies are tracking me down, as opposed to believing that someone who has not even been born is a "being"…a soul…a life. I've got to be kidding. Right?

Can I truly prove to you that Jake and God were not angry with me, but were actually there with me, in me, around me…just hanging out for any and all conversations, questions, problems, joys, tears…anything I cared to share with them?

Is Love that big?

What do you think?

***

I need to make very, very clear here that God has ***never*** communicated to me in any way that having the abortion was the right thing for me to do. Also as profoundly, God has ***never*** communicated to me that it was the wrong thing for me to do, or that I didn't have a right to the choice I made. My experiences and dialogue with God have in no way made me feel or think that I am condemned to eternal damnation because of my having the abortion. A not-so-secret secret in God's universe lies within accepting and living that paradox. Noah drank, David killed, Samson womanized, Paul persecuted...or so I have been reminded. We all come from and to God with mistakes made, some lie lived. We are loved unconditionally which allows us choice, our personal free will, always in our life. God's will for us is our will for ourselves. Our personal hells arise when we are choosing fear for ourself and not love for ourSelf. I gave Up to God and the Unseen around me on that Sabbath afternoon in May. It is quite possible I would not have written any of this down if Jake had not been conceived to start with so that he could show up in my life later; as a birth day Gift. Can you imagine? I couldn't have dreamt this Up. If God—Yahweh, Allah, the Source, Tao, Spirit, Infinite Intelligence...pick one...fight the semantics if you can—I could no longer—if the Higher Power surrounding me had not placed in front of me what was possible, I could not have opened my wings and flown off the ledge I flew off of that particular birth day.

Knowledge is power.

You can't disagree with that, can you? That short statement is Truth.

It is also Truth that there is no going backward to an unknowing of a *know ledge;* you cannot jump back to the cliff's ledge once jumped off. I realized, it became real to me, and I was finally willing to accept, believe—TO KNOW—that we are *ALL* surrounded by the Unseen and can communicate with *It* any time, any where we wish. The biggest leap is in accepting the *know ledge* that *the "thoughts" that run around in your mind are not necessarily in that moment yours alone. If you are coming from a place of your Highest Thoughts, Ideals, Truths, the place of Highest Love, then you are being helped, communicated with, and shown the Right Way...Always.*

This new found *know ledge* to me was much like it must have felt when more and more people in the world came to know, if they gave it any thought at all, that the earth was not flat; it was round. In that moment, it didn't change where they got their food, or how one took care of dirty clothes, but it completely changed where mankind knew it could travel to, which led to the next evolutionary step. It made new possibilities we found to be true explode and explode with, until "that time," unheard of intellectual, physical, and spiritual depth.

I continued reading in Neale and God's *Conversations with God, Book 3* that afternoon, and it changed my life forever. If you have not already enjoyed it, I wish for you the treasure found in the Holy words and the truths that are transcribed by Neale in the *Conversations with God* dialogues. I do not intend to put any more of their dialogue in this book. I have already perhaps used more than you might think I should, but I needed you to see how all the pieces start fitting together: the thoughts, the Holy words, the music, the colors, the summer arriving along with the butterfly. The *All* surrounded me and sent me forth flying amongst the rainbows.

Jake was, is, and always will be "around" me, and guess what? He, too, was just now getting started communicating with me. He began with fireworks, then moved on to Christmas ornaments, and finally rocks...and upon those rocks I have built my faith in God, Spirit, Tao, the Source, Allah, Yahweh...Absolute Love.

However, you can judge for yourself...as you will.

***

A couple of weeks after I had received my birthday card picture of Jake, I was sitting on the back steps at my home—same place I had been sitting crying with the moon the night Gary died. It was a few weeks after my birthday—June 2001—on a beautifully blue-skied summer morning. My two boys had left about five minutes before to go down the street

125

to play with one of the neighborhood kids. I was sitting, taking a deep breath deciding what I needed to do next—work on one of my graphics projects or finish cleaning the dishes, when a thought pops into my head…"You need to go check on my brothers."

What?…brothers?

"Mornin'," I heard in my head. He went on, "I said you need to go down and check on my brothers."

I had finally gotten to the point that when these kinds of thoughts came into my head from what seemed "nowhere," I did as I was "told." I stood up and started walking down our driveway toward the neighbor's house. I was a few yards down the street when I heard it…a familiar sound to most in the world…pop, pop, pop….

"Thanks, Jake!" I didn't hesitate thanking him in that moment…I knew he was right. The neighborhood kid my sons had gone to play with had been known to have a fascination with fireworks, and he didn't always think it was necessary to have parents around when shooting them off. At some point each June, the noise of bottle rockets, firecrackers, and various pyrotechnical "stuff" would start going off on our street. My boys at this time were not allowed to be around him when he was lighting any kind of fireworks by himself and that is where they were.

I heard another pop, pop as I turn the corner into this kid's driveway. At that moment, my two boys are, fortunately for them, still on this side of a fence that enclosed a field of pine trees. They were not allowed to cross over and be on the other side because a dog that didn't always take kindly to children ran loose in this field. They saw me coming and immediately took on the deer-in-the-headlights faces that I have come to know and love in the last several years…it screams out, "Oh, I am sooooo busted by her."

Another couple of seconds pass as I am walking up the driveway and here comes their buddy, crossing back over the fence from the field he had just shot off bottle rockets in, when he saw me. He knew as well that he was not supposed to shoot off any pyrotechnical "stuff" when my sons were around. He ran past me screaming, "I hate this," as he went running into his house.

For the rest of that summer, when my sons took off to play somewhere with their friends, I always thanked Jake for watching out for them. I would ask him to let me know if someone was in danger in some way. I started being told in my thoughts, "They'll be home in ten minutes," and I would look at the clock. Sure enough, ten minutes later I would hear one of them coming in through the door..."Moooooom, I'm hungry."

There was an afternoon that a group of boys were riding bikes and they were late checking in with me. I went to Jake in my thoughts, "What's going on?"

I heard back, "Nothing, a bike chain came off and they are fixing it."

Several minutes later they were all standing in our kitchen getting drinks. I asked the boys, "Whose bike chain came off?"

They all got this incredulous look on their faces and somebody asked, "How'd you know that?" Their ages ranged from eight to ten and I couldn't very well say, "Well, this 'dead' son of mine helps keep me informed about his brothers' comings and goings," now, could I?

In my head I heard, "Look at their hands."

Then I hear, "Tell them all their greasy hands are a 'dead' give away." I giggled the whole time I was saying it to them.

***

Jake became, and to this day is, a great comfort to me. At that time, however, even with all the tidbits of knowledge he would give me about "his brothers," I still questioned it all.

127

How could I not? The Christmas season of 2001 and the first couple of months into the New Year made me stop doing that forever. But first we had to make it through the "Fall" of 2001.

By the 11th of September 2001, most Americans, and many in the world, were again shown what it was like to face Fear...with or without Love. As I have come to try to grasp it, an extraordinary group of Heros...incredible human beings, gave the history of our time priceless Gifts...each and every One of them.

All generations have given humanity some profound Gift born out of enormous pain. This generation is no different. The rest of the world and I have been shown what True Honor is, yet again. God's mirror of courage and love was reflected to all of us by hundreds of men and women as they walked into two very tall buildings to do whatever was necessary to help the thousands trying to get out. As I sat crying my soul out on our kitchen floor that Tuesday morning, I knew I had been shown what strength of Love for your fellow man looked like. The sacred Strength to do what is right was shown to me by everyOne that was on a plane they themselves brought down into a farm field in Pennsylvania...priceless Gifts we can in no way truly repay.

By comparison, my choosing love over fear, my choosing to tell you of Jake and my mistakes in life is like my choosing between walking through my flower gardens or weeding them. If I can help one person that lost someone that day by coming to KNOW, not hope for, not have faith in, but to KNOW that their loved one is not gone, but only a "thought" away from them, sitting right there with them now as they read this. If they themselves prove to themselves through their own "Dialogue" with the husband, wife, son, daughter, mom, dad...if just one person learns to "read" the eternal language and dialogue between the Seen and Unseen of God's universe because of reading about these experiences of mine, then I have passed on my gift to give. This is my attempt to do so most humbly with the help of the role models of Love's courage gifted to all of us September 11 of 2001.

***

That morning my brother John was setting up for a meeting on the 23d floor of the World Trade Center Marriott that connected the two towers.

No kidding.

You would think someone who not nine months before had been in a horrendous car accident that almost took his "life" would have had enough grief for a year, but life doesn't always work that way, does it? John spent the night of September 10, 2001 having dinner with a friend at the Windows on the World restaurant at the top of the World Trade Center. The morning of the 11th he was early setting up the meeting room for his presentation and decided to go down across the street and get a cappuccino at Starbucks. As he walked out of the lobby of the Marriott, the first plane slammed into the Tower above him. He was not physically hurt; however, emotionally he lived through a waking, walking nightmare, as did everyone in New York City that day and for most of us, a long time to come.

I had no idea he was traveling in New York City. My mother calls me about 20 minutes after the second plane hits the second tower to tell me that John is somewhere in the middle of all the unbelievable horror the world began to watch unfold over their televisions.

I was already on the floor, crying, praying…just trying to absorb what was happening when the phone rang. Mom told me that Jacquelyn *had* heard from John right after the planes hit, but not since. She would let me know.

I immediately begged the Unseen around me to tell me what was going on with John. God, please tell me. I hear in my thoughts, "He is alive…he is okay…but he is going through a literal Hell right now. He is going to survive, trust that." It was shortly afterward the buildings started collapsing and there wasn't much left to trust in except my faith in the Unseen God wrapped tight around me.

About three hours later, John was able to reach Jacquelyn again and let her know he was okay. We were so totally devastated for so many families, but we were also incredibly grateful to still have John with our family.

And yes, he should write a book.

I don't in any way wish to cause any more sorrow to those who lost so much that fall day, so I think I have said more than enough about that time in our history. This book is not in any way meant to take advantage of that suffering. That moment will live forever, as all major evolutionary events do, whether physical, intellectual, or emotional—as a pivotal moment that forever changes the perspective we all share of our life on earth.

***

Jake would next say a real time, real life Hello to me at Christmas of 2001. Perhaps it will no longer surprise you to know that he "showed Up" at the Christmas Pool Tournament party at John and Jacquelyn's that year.

See how far we've come?

It was mid-December, the Christmas season and the day before John and Jacquelyn's annual party. I was heading outside to get the mail when Jake came into my thoughts. "Hey, Mom, you have a special card in today's mail. It's part of a gift I have for you."

To tell you the truth, I had worked hard **not** to think about him, so it surprised me. So many other things to think about that year for all of us...it wasn't that difficult for me to keep my mind occupied with other things. So much sorrow in the world, so many people lost, so many just wanted to skip the holidays altogether.

On a different level, I honestly wasn't sure I was ready to go through my "first" Christmas believing I had a "son" that wasn't "dead" and gone. Talk about an upside down dilemma during the holidays. When I heard his "thought" in my head, I stopped myself from walking and started getting choked up. To him in my thoughts I almost cried, To have even the "thought" of you with me this year is such an incredibly powerful gift. Last Christmas I would have said it was impossible. I am not sure I can handle conversing with you right now...and please don't call me mom, you know it makes me sad...I gave up that privilege.

"And one more time, no you did not. Please, don't get upset, just go get the mail."

There was only one Christmas card in the mailbox that day mixed in with bills and junk. Considering it was the holidays, there wasn't much there. Then I noticed the card was from a close friend's mother. The week before, I had sent her our Christmas card for the first time and this was her first Christmas card to us. I opened it smiling. She is a wonderful woman with a very deep and abiding Christian faith. The card she sent that year had a touching illustration at the top of it with Joseph leading a pregnant Mary riding on a donkey into the town of Bethlehem. Below the illustration was printed the Christmas Story (Luke 2:4-7, RSV):

And Joseph also went up from Galilee, from the city of Nazareth, to Judea, to the city of David, which is called Bethlehem...And while they were there, the time came for her to be delivered. And she gave birth to her first-born son and wrapped him in swaddling cloths, and laid him in a manger, because there was no place for them in the inn.

I wanted to fall on my knees then and there and just get swallowed by all the grief and regret at how I handled my own pregnancy. Some gift...the tears were going to come long and hard that day except for this next thought....

"No, no, no...Please don't do that," Jake said. "No, no...sadness is not what this is about. Giving is what this time of year is about; the giving of life, Mary giving birth. You are giving me birth in ways few ever conceptualize, much less believe and know to be true...You with this conversation in our thoughts...that is giving me Life with you. Don't be sad. That is worth celebrating. Wait 'til after the party tomorrow night and we shall see how you feel about a gift from me to you."

I thought of all the tremendous losses that year in the world and my problems were so small in comparison. I let the sadness go...We shall see, I thought to myself... We?... hmmmmmmm.

***

Twenty-four hours later found me heading to Louisville with Martin to go to my brother's house for our annual Christmas gathering. I was so excited on the way down. This was the first time since August that I had been happy and looking forward to a party, and would you believe it was this particular party? Imagine that.

About a half hour after we arrived, I was standing in the kitchen helping get some food ready when one of the guys, Michael, came through the back door. He is, was, and always will be a very special friend to me. He was carrying some packages of food "stuff" and a gift bag that I knew contained his Christmas ornament. Everyone brings a wrapped up Christmas ornament and toward the end of the party we each get to pick one to take home. We try to slip ours into the pile of ornaments to be exchanged without anyone seeing us so that we don't know whose wrapped, bowed, or bagged ornament is whose.

Hey, Jake, I thought, I think you are trying to help show me which bag contains the ornament from Michael. We don't have one from him yet...I would love that. Thanks.

"Let's just see what the evening brings," is the only response I get back in my head.

So I waited. The party yet again was such tremendous fun. It always is. Gary showed up in my thoughts a few times, helping me decide what pool shot to take, but I knew that my winning the pool tournament "with help" two years before was to make me aware of new possibilities, and very much a One-time use of energy and definitely not something that was going to "happen" every time this party came around.

The night started to wind down and several of the women, myself included, started to sit around the fireplace where we exchange the ornaments to take home. Many years this is my favorite time of the night. I remember the first party we had and a very special woman, Trisha, Tino's wife, had brought the first ornament I took home from this gathering. Trisha had picked out an exquisite angel that you could put a light under to illuminate on the tree. That angel had magnificently glowed on our tree for many years now. I always smile when I unwrap her each year. I cherish her as I do all the ornaments Martin and I have received from these glorious friends over the many years.

By the time it was my turn that night to select a package with our ornament for the year, there were three packages left. One was the gift bag Michael had walked in with, the one next to it was a beautifully wrapped box with a big bow on top, and the third was in another gift bag.

When there had been five packages left, and I knew my turn was coming and it looked like Michael's ornament was going to be available for me to choose, in my head I thought,

Thanks, Jake, for any help you gave me in noticing Michael walking in with his gift. We will now have an ornament from him to add to our collection.

"You may pick that gift if you want," I hear from Jake in my thoughts, "but the one I would like you to have is the one next to it, the box with the big bow. Am I here, Mom, really here to you, in this moment? Will you give me birth in yourself, Ann…in your Knowing? If you believe I exist, then pick the box next to Michael's bag. It is coming to you with my help, my blessings, and my Love."

What would you have done with those "thoughts" in your head?

It was my turn to pick and three packages were left. I picked the box with the big bow.

There were many wonderful ornaments that year. There were reindeer and Santas, stockings and wreaths; there was even a wonderful chrome Martini shaker with olives. The ornament that Michael had brought was of an adorable green frog in a pink ballet tutu. You had to smile when you looked at her. But the one I received was quite different.

The ornament I took home with me was the only ornament that night that had anything to do with the birth of Jesus…the only one…which struck me as I was looking at everyone else's ornaments when we got done with our ornament exchange. None of the others had a religious theme that year except for the ornament I was holding.

I had tears in my eyes when I opened the box. The only person looking at me while I was doing so was Julia. She is such a warm, loving, tremendously funny woman. I had a feeling this beautifully wrapped package had come from her and her equally tremendous husband, Bert. I was correct and so glad of that. I love them both very much and somehow it was right that whatever this ornament was, was coming from them.

When I saw what was in the box I knew Jake had helped. I pulled out a beautiful glass globe that had been hand painted from the inside out with a glorious illustration of Joseph leading a pregnant Mary on the same donkey riding into Bethlehem.

***

And then came the Rocks.

We as a species have evolved intellectually to a point where we now *know* something about a rock that would have been considered completely absurd 75 years ago. Truth can seem absurd. This *know ledge* we have now climbed, reached, and evolved to know as Truth is a know *ledge* that, once jumped off of, changes a civilization's direction much like the course change that arose when the *know ledge* that the earth was round, not flat, had reached critical mass and was jumped off of by most on this planet. Knowing that the earth was round, not flat, did not drastically alter overnight where someone got their food, or how they washed their dirty clothes, but it did forever change the discoveries humanity considered to be possible.

We are now at a time for another dawning of knowledge and I was shown this truth—through a rock. Sound crazy? Well you've come this far…just a little farther…please.

Any rock, held in any hand, is solid and just sits there unless some outside force moves it. Right?

Sort of.

The opposite is *also* true: a dichotomy in rock. That same solid, unmoving rock is made up of millions of particles that are in constant motion. Scientists are discovering that the particles that make up everything in our universe are constantly pulsating and there are spaces in between all the pulsating particles creating our world and us. We, as a species, are just now becoming aware of the full implications

135

of particled matter. It is no accident that we now discuss quantum, parallel, crystalline, and string universes. Scientifically we have been diving as deep as is possible into this physical realm by today's scientific and intellectual elite. I couldn't begin to understand, much less explain to you, all the scientific data, nor would I begin to insult your intelligence by trying to, but I do now know and completely accept that the stillness and solid nature of any and all things at some level is an *illusion* created by the movement of particles in space. Think of watching your favorite movie on a big screen. There are individual film cells flicked by you so fast there seems to be only constant moving images; thus, the name "motion picture." Moving pictures create the movie picture. We are now going digital and it isn't even individual film cells...it is billions of individual pixels. Think of them as moving, creative, illusory pixies. Everything—you, me, these words you are reading—is all created by constant motion and movement. The protons, neutrons, electrons, blah-blah-blah-trons surrounding you are pulsing at speeds so incredibly fast that we cannot "see" the movement with our eyes. Our sight is not designed to see incredibly tiny particles moving that fast. If we could do that, the Gig would be Up...it would all be over because we would see what is All around us. However, that is a discussion for another time.

This is not. The still and solid nature of all rocks, of everything around us, is an illusion created by movement and space.

In the *Conversations with God, Book 1*, God explains so eloquently and Neale transcribes perfectly what is called the Parable of the Rock.[1] It is as powerful as the Mustard Seed, the Prodigal Son, or any of the other Holy Parables I was raised up on from the Bible. After I had read the Parable of the Rock in Book 1, the lesson it teaches never really left me. The secrets of the Universe are held in a rock and I understood what was being explained when I first read it, but

I didn't fully comprehend its depth. My understanding kept delving deeper and deeper into the implications of this truth and the illusions in life as time passed.

One afternoon after the Christmas holidays, I was sitting alone just thinking about the Unseen flowing around me—invisible but very real, and the "real" visible world around me that wasn't as still as it appeared but was moving around me all the time…with spaces in between. It was a challenging and enlightening winter afternoon's meditative mental exercise.

"There is something for you up on the mantel," comes into my head.

Something?

"A rock. A small rock is sitting on your mantel for you."

A rock? Why in the world would a rock be on the mantle?

"I would like you to put it in your pocket for me and my brothers." And it wasn't until then that I knew these thoughts were from Jake.

I got up off the couch and looked around the mantle over our fireplace, and sure enough, there was a small, polished, triangular-shaped rock sitting behind one of the pictures that rested on our mantle.

Now how did that get there? I asked.

"Well, you do raise two boys, don't you?"

Any mother of boys knows that enough had been said. Boys "do" rocks. They carry them in their pockets, pick them up here and there, roll around in them. Now don't get me wrong, I was a "tom girl" growing up and I know that many girls enjoy playing with rocks, as well, but just about all boys at some point growing up collect, spit on to polish, carry in their pockets, and in general just "do" the rock thing.

"I would like you to carry that rock around with you in your pockets for a few days, if you don't mind," comes into my thoughts.

Okay, Jake, I would love to…this is a very pretty rock. Thanks for pointing it out to me, I thought back to him. It was actually a wonderful rock, as rocks go: shiny, polished and smooth. It was then I started to wonder where it had come from in the first place and how it had found its way onto our mantle. I asked all the guys in my house if they had put it there. I got the stereotypical "not me" from all of them. I explained to the boys that I was in no way mad at them for any reason; I actually liked the rock a lot and just wondered how it came to be on top of the fireplace. They both stuck to their guns…"It wasn't me, Mom. Don't know where it came from." Martin didn't have a clue either as to how it got into the house…hmmmmmm?

So for the next several days I started carrying around a rock in my jeans pocket and believe it or not, it was great fun. I started to realize that I had a habit of putting my hands in my pockets a lot more than I thought I did and because of that, having the rock made me smile a lot more because of all the times my hands seemed to end up in my pockets. A couple of afternoons after I first started carrying it around, one of my sons turned back the clock by about nine years and became a two year-old in the middle of a tantrum. He had just about hit my zone of impatience, which is a place my boys are well aware of. This "zone" is not a very big place and it takes a while to get there, but after you arrive you realize two things: the atmosphere is lousy and you don't want to stay long. My son had just about arrived in that no man's zone as I was angrily walking toward him to put him into a "time out" when, without thinking about it, I put my hand in my pockets and felt the rock.

It stopped me in my tracks…the rock is an illusion.

The situation I found myself in with my son at that moment was, as well.

The power of the parable…the secret in the rock.

My anger at him dissipated in the time it took for me to rub my fingers twice around that rock in my pocket. That, in and of itself, surprised me. I looked at the situation I found myself in at that moment with him and it all completely flipped on me. Within the next couple of seconds, I was able to use humor and turn the whole situation completely around, so that we were both hugging before you could say "let's rock around the clock" three times. I thought that was powerful enough, but once again things were just getting started for me, and would you believe, this time it was with the Rocks in my life, not in my head?

***

During the winter of 2002, American soldiers were invading a country that seemed to be made of not much more than mountainous rock, at least that is how it looked from the images coming across the television. The United States invaded Afghanistan.

This was before we invaded Iraq—i raq—a rock— hmmmm, imagine that, another rock that was more than it appeared to be. A coincidence? Anyway, at this time we were only in Afghanistan.

One afternoon I was watching a report on the war, when this face came across the screen and my heart skipped a beat and then started beating really fast and that led to an intake of breath…you know those moments… something good or bad happens in a moment that takes your breath away. This was a good moment and a very surprising one.

What took my breath away was that this guy on my TV screen looked like I would have pictured Jake to look if he were alive in this physical reality. This guy was being interviewed on a news program as a specialist on some aspect of Afghanistan. I ran to get the picture of Jake I had been given and then compared it to this guy who was talking about his experiences with the Afghanistan people and fighters. The picture with Jake, the mountains in the background…oh, my God. This guy on TV was an American—in his late twenties, early thirties; a writer and published author; and God help me, at the very least, could have been passed off as Jake's brother.

The physical similarities blew me away. I was so happy and so sad all at the same time. I know this might sound very weird, but I have probably raised the "bar" on weirdness in your life now and that is just the way it is. I was mesmerized by the looks of this young man, by the way he sounded, what he said. And then the "thoughts" started in my head. Not many, as it turned out, but not many were needed.

"Pay attention to his name. You will see him again, hear him again for a while. He will pop in and out of your life in the next few weeks," comes into my mind.

Only a little while?…and doesn't he look like Jake? Or is it just me?

"Annie, you are beginning to know the Truth that on the Spiritual level there is only One of us, we are all connected, we ARE ALL ONE. This young man is going to help to give you a gift. Just listen for him, watch for him in the next couple of weeks."

Well, needless to say, I did just that and of course, he did show Up several times over the next few weeks. I certainly looked out for him. Most often it was at night while he was being interviewed on news programs about the Afghani fighters. Then one morning I was working in my studio and I had a program from NPR—National Public Radio—on and I heard that the next hour was going to be an interview with this same young man.

I heard that he was next on the radio and my heart flipped. "Wow, this guy is getting around…how cool is that! I love this; thanks, God, very much."

"Don't thank Me, thank him, and yes, he is getting around because he is working very hard to get the truth of the Afghanistan people out into the world. Not the Taliban's terror, but the story of the frustrating and proud struggle of the Afghani people themselves fighting the war that different countries of the world and the Taliban have waged on them for decades. He is getting that message out. He also has a gift for you today, something important to say that you need to hear. Listen Up."

And with those thoughts in my head, I turned away from the computer screen I was working at and went to turn on our stereo. I knew I needed to sit and listen to the entire interview, so I moved to the living room. The program would last an hour and I figured I might as well listen to it through decent speakers, as opposed to the small radio I had in my studio. The interviewer was a woman I love to listen to and this young man was her only guest.

In this particular interview, he said many of the same things I had heard him saying over the last several weeks, but this time he was able to respond with quite a bit more depth. He wasn't trying to get all of the questions answered in 15 minutes or less. He and the interviewer had an hour to discuss his experiences, beliefs, feelings, and his story.

I sat and patiently listened to all he had to say…again. This was a good guy! The kind of young man I am trying to raise my boys to be. He was doing whatever he could to help his world. Here was a young man to be proud of.

Then I started to get antsy because the hour was almost up and I still hadn't heard anything that I would personally consider a gift to me. I was beginning to get frustrated because I had projects waiting. Then the interviewer asked a question that perked up my ears. He was asked about his religious beliefs. You could hear in his voice that he was not comfortable about the "religion" question. He didn't attend any church regularly, nor did he consider himself affiliated with any particular religious dogma. Then the interviewer asked about something that he carried around with him. "Maybe religion is the wrong word; perhaps it would be better to say spiritual. I say that because in my notes here it says you carry something around in your pockets."

"Just a rock or two," he replied. "I carry rocks around in my pocket."

He went on to explain that he has a collection of rocks that are special to him for various reasons. He had gotten each of them in different places in the world and he couldn't explain exactly why, but he always carried at least one of them around with him in his pockets…"just" a rock.

"We're gonna rock this town, rock it inside out
We're gonna rock this town, rock it 'til they
scream and shout…."[2]

That golden oldie just came on my radio as I am first writing this section down. Imagine that happening, circling around two years after the above experience occurred.

Then it was God's turn with rocks.

***

Early that spring I was working in my art studio with the radio playing while I was looking at a map of Indiana to find a small town where a prospective client was located and I noticed that there was a place called St. Paul, Indiana. I had never heard of it before.

"Yes, and I want you to go there," comes into my head, very quick and very adamant.

At this point the name Paul had been showing Up in my life for a long time and I had really started noticing that fact. I have a friend Paul who is a brother to me like Gary, and I speak of him on the first page of this book. It was Paul who first called to tell me of Gary's "death." He is always with me in my heart.

During this time I kept being introduced to guys named Paul. You know, in business or out with friends and we would run into someone they knew. "Annie," they would say, "I would like you to meet my friend, Paul." My sons have a close friend named Paul I adore. The writings of Saint Paul kept running through my life before, during, and after my brother's accident and again at this time. The fact that Saint Paul had been known as Saul of Tarsus until he "saw the light" was not lost on me either. So, in my head on this Monday morning, I asked God a question...You want me to go to St. Paul, Indiana?

"Yes, it is time for you to go there."

Right now? You want me to go right now, today? I really didn't have that much work, but it was a Monday morning and to go on what sounded to me like a "Sunday drive" on a Monday morning seemed like a waste of time. These thoughts are going on in my head and then I think, Besides, I don't have the extra money this week to pay for the gas. Two bucks is all I've got right now in my wallet and I'm not going to get money out of the bank this week if I can help it. God, you know that...I can't do it right now, I'm sorry.

"Don't be sorry. I will make you a deal," comes in my head.

A deal, with *You?*...hmmmmm.

"Yes, a deal. You go buy a ticket right now and if you win any money at all, you take it and you go to St. Paul— today, this morning."

A ticket? What ticket?????? God, what are you talking about?

And then through the radio waves it comes...the beginning of a commercial for a new lottery ticket...called Cash Blues.

I swear to God.

I was being led once again by a color…this time by a ribbon of blue. I dropped everything I was doing, grabbed my purse with the two dollars in it, and went up to the corner drug store where they sold lottery tickets. I walked in and purchased one Cash Blues lottery ticket and stood there scratching off the silver to see if I had won anything.

I came out of the drug store shaking, with ten bucks in my hand, and a giggling phrase being played over and over in my mind….

"Annie, you've just won the Cash Blues lottery…what are you going to do next?"

I am going…oh, God…I am going to St. Paul.

***

Located southeast of Indianapolis, Indiana along I-74, St Paul is about 45 minutes away. I got on the interstate and headed in that direction. About half hour later my gas light came on. I had been so blown away by winning $10 with the Cash Blues ticket that I had forgotten to get gas before I left town.

Great, Ann, just great, I think to myself.

"It is okay," comes into my head. "You have enough gas to get to St. Paul. There is a station there. You can gas Up…don't you just love that part?!"

Just then a commercial starts on the radio for BP Connect. The BP stands for British Petroleum, and the word Connect speaks for itself, doesn't it? BP Connect is the name of an international chain of gas stations and I felt reassured that I would at least make it to some kind of gas station without being stranded on the interstate in the middle of nowhere with no one else with me. The signs for St. Paul showed up a short while later; and would you believe, the exit is numbered 123?

"See, there? That wasn't so hard. Some things are as simple as 1, 2, 3," I hear as I turn off the exit.

Yeah, well I need gas, now, if at all possible, I replied in my thoughts. As I came to the end of the ramp there was a sign to St. Paul and I turned as shown. A mile down I came into St. Paul, which is a very, very small town. Actually, the term farming village would better describe it. And there in the middle of this village was a BP Connect; and as it turns out, it was the only gas station in town.

I pulled in and put $10 of gas into the tank. After I had paid and gotten back in to the van I thought, Okay, now what? It was then I noticed the little sign sticking out of the grass across the street. It read *Hidden Paradise Campground* with an arrow pointing to go to the left.

"That's where you are to go," I heard in my thoughts.

Thanks, I said. I probably could have guessed that one on my own, and with a huge smile on my face I turned left out of the gas station. I drove about a mile or so down the road and found the signs directing me into Hidden Paradise Campground. I had no idea what I would find when I got there, and after driving around for a few minutes I still wasn't sure. As I drove down a winding road, I realized this was a charming spot in the middle of Indiana that you would never just run into if you didn't know it was there. I wasn't sure what I was supposed to do. Then I came around a bend and you could see the lake. It wasn't very big, maybe six acres in size, but it was lovely. As I came around another bend, I noticed a parking area to the right of the lake and I pulled in and parked.

I got out of the car, stretched for a moment, and started walking across the street to the lake and a round picnic table that was sitting empty. There was no one around, although I did hear a chainsaw going somewhere in the distance. There had to be someone around. It was then I noticed the small wooden sign hanging on a post near the table. It read Dream Lake.

"This is an old rock quarry," I heard in my thoughts. "Lots of rocks have come out of here, and dreams."

I was surrounded by nature, water, and rock. It was incredible. I just kept smiling and the calmness I had learned to recognize as a Oneness with the All washed over me. I saw that a dock stretched out into the lake on the opposite side of where I was standing. "Drive over that way, please. You needed to see the name of this lake, but now you should go sit over there for a while." I didn't need to be told twice. At that moment it looked like the most perfect spot in the world to me. I realized I was looking at another very humble place that held the power of the universe within its boundaries.

I sat on the dock with my shoes off and my feet in the water.

Well, God, I suppose it's time for me to go back to church.

"You think so? Which church?"

Ah, now there's the question.

"Ann, has it not yet occurred to you?"

Has *what* not yet occurred to me?

"You never leave my Church; none of you do, ever! You only tell yourselves you do. You are in My Church right now, right here. Did I lead you to a building, or an organization? You think you are separate from Me, so you go into buildings to be with Me. Some are exquisitely designed areas and others are the most humble of spaces. All can generate communication with me, but it doesn't matter *where* you are, rather *how* you are in any given space. *When you are truly One with Me, you know we are never apart, for we are always a part of one another*. This is taught by the churches, synagogues, mosques, temples, shrines, etc., created to worship the divine God. They are *all* wonderful places to help others and yourself; and in those places you can increase the

146

power of the common union between Us...the *communion* between Us. Religious groups can be the best way to recruit and organize people to help other people...but have I led you today to the inside of a church? You may practice any religion you wish, any time you wish, and it would be wonderful for both of us, but you don't have to limit our friendship that way. You cannot limit Me that way. Please know that a friendship with Me, a common union with Me, a communion with Me, a communication with Me, often doesn't happen until you leave the buildings and organizations with all the rules and regulations behind and see Me, hear Me, feel Me for What and Who I am. For I am simply and magnificently the All; I am with you always, in All ways, and whether you understand that or not does not change what Is.

"The beloved Jesus taught outside the buildings of his time to teach the know *ledge* that what you do to the least of his brothers and sisters you do to Him. He knew and was born Aware that there is only One of us. His ledge was one of the hardest ever climbed by any human being. He KNEW and LIVED that what you do to and for each other, you do to yourself...*for whatever you do to someone else is done to you*. That is Sacred Law and golden advice! We are ALL ONE and He was willing to die...willing to give His All to give you that holy knowledge. We are all in this together and life does not end after death...the world has been living, loving, and learning of Him and his Way ever since.

"The beloved Buddha, after leaving his gilded buildings of wealth behind, became rich with the knowledge of the Universal Way...the power that lies *within* each person...and the world began to listen to the power of One that is inherent in ALL men and women and walk the Way that He lived.

"The beloved Muhammad taught outside the structures of his time and has been studied, read, and worshipped ever since for the deep and profound knowledge he brought to mankind. He brought the Way of Allah, the most Holy One.

"The beloved Abraham was one of the first to teach of the One, Elohim. He lived the love; spoke the knowledge; taught the faith in, of, and through the Way of the One God. His Way is ancient, honored, and Sacred."

God continued, "There are many others throughout history who have shown everyone the Way and the power of One person: Martin Luther King, Jr.; Mother Teresa; Gandhi; just a very small number of the men and women of your time who not only taught, but lived that we are all connected to each other, we are all One in this world, forever without end, Amen. They understood and were deeply committed to the fact that living peacefully with one another with respect and integrity was the best Way for everyOne. They knew that regardless of where they were in any given moment, they were, are, and always will be with, in, and a part of Me. Life is how you *look* at it. *We are never apart from each other, for we are ALWAYS A PART OF EACH OTHER..* The change in your 'thoughts' can be that subtle, that simple, and that evolutionary."

"You have brought me to a place called Paradise, yet again, God, and this time *I do know* that I am in one of Your gardens...I LOVE THAT PART!" I shouted out loud to the space around me.

In my thoughts came, "And you, My loved One, have become a butterfly in My garden. I am honored by you."

I was so moved by this dialogue I couldn't answer, not even silently in my head...all I could do was nod yes as the tears streamed.

"This Uni Verse we are now in is one Garden, one Paradise...Our Paradise. You were taught growing up that I got angry at some of my greatest creations, human Beings, and then kicked you out of Paradise, My garden of Eden. You are beginning to know after all the experiences you have had,

148

that that simply isn't Truth. I never kicked anyone out of any Paradise...I love you All—*Absolutely*. You are becoming aware and making real to yourself that Eden is a state of mind, not a location. That is truth. I did not banish anyone out of any garden. However, you do walk out, regularly...in your mind and with your hearts. You need only walk back in, anytime, anywhere, any Way you wish. That is the part that I love! If mankind really needs a place to call Paradise, then you should know that your entire planet Earth is Eden. Imagine both words starting with the letter E...like Eternal, Everlasting, Evolutionary, and Enlightened. You think after all it took for Earth to exist that 'Eden' would be found in just one location? Travel from Tahiti to the Tigress River by Way of Lake Tahoe...just a minute sample of the glorious places created on your planet for any and all to enjoy. What becomes of *Our* Paradise is, in part, dependent on what humanity chooses to do with it."

Oh, God, I thought, it makes me so sad to think of what some people think we have a right to do with this planet. Mother Earth is sick and we have made her that way!

"That is true, but don't be sad today...not on My time...let's lighten Up, shall we? A little Enlightenment is good for the soul." I was giggling again. "Annie, right now, in this moment, you know you are surrounded by Me, don't you? What you are beginning to realize is that never changes and you are also surrounded by my posse...so stick 'em Up!"

Humor...getting used to God using humor can take a while. I don't know why; I mean, when you climb to the ledge I was sitting on at this moment, you start to realize Who created humor in the First Place. But we are trained in this life to think that anything to do with God must be in some way controlled, dignified, and quiet...or else it must be the other swing of the pendulum: loud, burning, and huge.

This was "just" funny. Now, I was laughing and the tears stopped. It was the beginning of an incredible dialogue between my Creator and me that day.

Your posse?

"My child, Jesus sits beside you right now and at all times. The friend you grew Up with is there with you *always*, to *re*mind you of the importance of the knowledge that it is through the loving of others that you, in truth, love yourSelf. That is One Way. Buddha sits with you *always* to remind you that there is someone who is just as important as everyone else...and that someone is YOU. You can love another only to the extent you will love yourSelf. You are in charge of your path and how you walk it in your life...and all ways eventually lead to the Source of All life.

"Abraham and Muhammad stand in friendship together, arms entwined, *always*, to give you the gift of rock over time...the sands of time...an oasis of rock for all ages. They both teach of the One Way. They have all related My truths on the power in the knowledge that WE ARE ALL ONE. Historical knowledge behind you, behind them, pushing all of Us forward...that is Our evolution. All Ways lead to the One and the One leads to all Ways...*Always*."

But now what do I do? I asked God.

"Now that you see the Light, you be a light unto the darkness," replied God. That thought lit Up my mind, my heart, and my soul...and in that moment I knew of Purpose.

God continued, "There are millions of butterflies like you in the world—flying with and in love, bringing the Light to all the rest. Some of you know you are butterflies and some do not. Some haven't 'looked' at it in that way, but you are all bearers of the Light through the living of love. We are reaching for another Ledge and that reaching will allow all of Us to arrive at a critical mass of peace and serenity on the earth."

I started giggling and God asked what was funny.

Don't You know?...You read my thoughts, I replied.

"Yes, but it is soooooo much more fun for both of us if you say it out loud. Be it, live it, do it, experience the All in everything so I can enjoy it with you."

Well, I do end up going to mass...pun fully intended to you. I love these full circles you swirl around me. How gloryUs is that?

"And you, my butterfly," God replied, "are beginning to fly and dance to the Way of Love."

God......*Beloved* God
Allah
Jehovah
Yahweh
Elohim
The Great Spirit
The Holy Mystery
Divine Creator
Sacred Matrix
Infinite Intelligence
The Source
The Most Holy One
Stood All around me,
Leading in One Dance....
One Way...All Ways
Together, Forever, amen....
One for All and All for One....
you take the high Way
and I'll take the low Way...
and I'll be in Paradise afore ye....
We giggled the afternoon a Way....
in a common union...
a Communion, with,
amongst and between
All the parts of One.

Then it was time for *me* to get started. First it was the poetry. How many poems do you think you had to write to get through grade school and high school? I figure I had to write about a dozen...a little more, maybe; six or seven in grade school, about the same in high school. I took psychology in college so that was about it for me. A few days after this trip to St. Paul, I was sitting thinking about how gloryUs that day had been and the "thought" came into my head, "Try to write about the next time you go there."

Hmmmmm, I thought to myself. Well, let's see....It took just a few minutes for me to write the following:

Anticipation in Blue

Moments of time nearing
exact date would present itself
tied in ribbons of blue

They knew where

A place to be free
to speak, to touch, to Dance
under, through, with the Sun

Warmth around the corner
shamrocks in the air, flowers waking
the heartbeat of the Earth quickens
as Spring herSelf is born

Loose ends pull
with the illusion of rocks
Odd makers of the world
wouldn't give them a chance in hades

But, heaven
the Unseen surrounds

They are led by the Sun.
A rainbow of ribbons sent to guide
to a lake of dreams discovered;
a paradise hidden
except to those awakened
to the possibilities
of the Way it can Be . . . .

I finished writing these phrases and I had this wonderful rush, this joyful creative "high" for an hour after that. Is the poem good? No, not really, but it was fun to write it. What I didn't expect was for more poetry to come, and come into my head quickly...and some of it, in my humble opinion, was fairly good.

A few days after *Anticipation in Blue*, I was sitting in my wild flower bed and the "thought" comes, "Write Me another poem about what you were just thinking." I had been looking at my wild flowers and thinking of some of the crazy names people have given wild flowers...so I wrote:

The Dutchman hung up his breeches
and the tulips puckered up.
The dog's tooth pierced my violets
while the Sun poured butter into cups.

I started giggling again...especially when thinking about two lips puckering up...and within the next 15 minutes...the rest of this filled my head, and I wrote....

Little Jack in his pulpit
spoke of a spirited soul renewed.
The bells rang out their splendor
painted an exquisite shade of blue.

Spring beauty wrapped around me.
May apples danced with the wind.
Blue-eyed Mary sat and wondered
about the Magic that God does send.

That is entitled *The Tulips Puckered Up*. By the time the
third poem, *Divine Dichotomy of a Rock*, came meandering
into my head and was written in less than half an hour, I was
once again a mazed.

Divine Dichotomy of a Rock

Any rock
held in any hand
solid mass, unmoving

Is it?

Infinite particles
in constant motion
with spaces between
Illusion created

Any rock
held in any hand

Is it a solid mass, unmoving?

Evolution of thought in a species led to question…
Which is truth?
Led to answer
Both….
Divining who created the dichotomy in the First Place
Led to Wisdom….

They kept coming, the poems. For the season of a butterfly the poetry swirled around me. With help from the Unseen floating through my thoughts, I wrote close to three dozen between March and November. As it turned out—who knew?—some of them work quite well with this book. Imagine that.

This is my first book. What do you think?

I am not alone in my thoughts when I write, and I did start to realize that early on. I am a fairly intelligent, clever woman, but I never had a desire to write. I began to realize that I had become literally *inspired*…moved in spirit…and when that happens the *inspiration* is released in some form; one aspires to create some type of artistry with the glorious energy that seems to come through you.

Gary, needless to say, was in my "thoughts" that Autumn on the third anniversary of his death. I was sitting by a window crying when he came into my thoughts and said, "Annie, honey, it is time for you to consider writing down some of what has happened…put down on paper some of what we have experienced."

Oh, I couldn't do that, Gary…I'm not a writer.

"Really?" he says. "Take a minute and reread *The Circle Weaver, Trap Door to Sorrow, A Paradise Grown*, or *Fantasea*. Somebody wrote them. It seems to me I watched you do it."

Gary, I thought, you know I had help with those. Besides, I wouldn't know where to start.

"Start with what happened three years ago today. It will help you heal, I promise."

And so on a November day in 2002, I wrote the first chapter of this book. I cried and laughed my way through the first chapter that day; and I have cried and laughed my Way through the rest. The experiences, the pieces of the puzzle I had lived kept working their way through my head and I would get them written down. I started to see the healing gift that reading my journey of a caterpillar becoming a butterfly might bring to someOne... perhaps to you.

I chose to continue writing these chapters. It took me almost two years between kids, marriage, work, life and the living of it...to finish this book. It is my choice to give it a Way...out to where you are.

A Paradise Grown

Quickly He bent over
perhaps for the zillionth time.
Caring for the Life around him
as if creating fine wine.
A hummingbird floated nearby,
lunching with the Trumpet vine.

Carefully He chose colors.
Which one to pick and where,
like an old Master's landscape created
skillfully painted layer upon layer.
Selecting from Nature's infinite palette
showing great expertise, subtle flair.

Slowly He stood up,
critiquing the beauty He'd sown.
Were the textures mixed correctly,
with the right spacing, proper tone?
From afar I sat watching, knowing,
a Paradise this Gardener had grown.

*The heart forever
beating strength of inner truth;
the living of Love.*

Chapter X
Choice

Pick a color.

Please.

Any color.

Thank you.

Now, pick a number.

Have it?

Good, remember what color and number *you* choose.

That is the story of my being a caterpillar and becoming a butterfly. It was after this *my* journey started to "take off"…pun fully intended to you. Reading this book may seem as if you have just won your own pool tournament and you didn't even know you were playing. The eight ball has been in charge and you just kept watching the Games unfold….

We are all Playing, every moment of Every Moment. It is your choice as to whether or not you choose to look at it that Way. You can do right now what many wonderful caterpillars do and hit the snooze button. It is a fine and completely respectable reaction; doesn't change what Is. Watch, listen, "see" what is *All* around you.

You always have the ability in your day-to-day life to communicate with God anytime, anywhere that you wish.

You may "talk, think and feel" with those who have "died." The Unseen already communicates with you. Our Creator uses Godsign – a language of the Divine – to speak to you everyday. The only thing stopping you from believing that Knowledge, is the "thought" we have all shared for so long that that just isn't possible.

What do I mean by saying that someone who is "dead" can communicate with you? How in the world could I say, much less explain, how God speaks to you? It is all around you, for you to choose, your decision.

I will give you an example.

I was with a woman named Rebecca one afternoon and had found out that her father had died and the first anniversary of his death was quickly approaching; in fact, it was only a few days away. She was a very warm and loving woman suffering from deep grief. She "just happened" to be wearing a bright yellow shirt that day and because I know to pay attention to the little things, I knew that yellow could be very important. Imagine that. We were with other people and I didn't want to make a big deal out of what I was going to say, so I went up to her and gave her a good long hug because she certainly needed one. I whispered in her ear that her father would say *Hi* to her using the color yellow.

"Oh, you think so?" she asked. "Thanks for saying that to me," she said, "but I'll be okay, really," and the conversation changed. We both lived in Indianapolis but were meeting in a town about an hour away from there. I drove back to Indy a couple of hours before she did because she had another meeting to go to that afternoon. On the way home, three different times I drove past huge fields of yellow wild flowers. Huge fields, not little fields but acres of yellow *easily* noticeable. It was early summer so it was too early for goldenrod, but something was blooming that was very yellow and there was lots of it. I was so happy, I thought surely she would notice these fields and at least smile at the coincidence.

A couple of weeks later, Rebecca and I met for another business meeting at her office in Indy. We had been talking for a while and the meeting was winding down. As she finished writing the last of her notes on a yellow legal pad, I asked her if she had noticed her Dad saying *Hi* with the color yellow.

"Oh no," she said, "but that is okay, I'm okay," and she patted me on the hand in a way that told me she thought I was a little more than weird. I walked out of her office and headed outside through the front doors of the building she entered and left every day. There, painted right in front of the entrance, were two very wide, very long bright yellow stripes painted for parking purposes. Depending on how you looked at it, if you looked at it at all, the yellow stripes formed an 11, which in certain circles is known to be a a number of awakening and what can be referred to as a "master" number. I smiled, then I laughed. In that moment her dad certainly said *Hi* to me and told me that he surrounds her every day with his love...her choice as to whether to see the Love being sent or not.

A couple of days after the "yellow stripes," I was meeting with two other women, Debbie and Sarah. Debbie had brought Sarah to talk with me because Sarah had been very sad for a long while. Sarah's mom had "died" after a long battle with cancer, and her boyfriend Scott had "died" unexpectedly from a heart attack. Both deaths had happened within a couple months of each other. Sarah was another warm and loving woman suffering from deep grief. She had, in a very short period of time, experienced both types of death of a loved one: long and drawn out, as well as short and tragic.

We were having a lunch meeting at a restaurant, during which I told them both of my beliefs that none of us ever dies...ever. I related a couple of my stories and then I suggested Sarah pick a color...any color. She wondered if she could pick two colors? "By all means, please do," I said to her. We started talking about the memories she had of both her mom and boyfriend. She asked if I thought they were okay. I told her that with the two colors she had chosen, they would say *Hi* and let her know that they were great. Right about then our lunch was served and we went on to talking about all kinds of things you would find three women talking about.

Toward the end of our meal, the waiter came to clear our plates. He went to pick up this little black "thing" on the table. I thought it was a black bead or rock of some kind. As the waiter reached to pick it up, Sarah said, "No! That is mine, thank you, but I am keeping that."

I looked at her and she said one of the colors she had picked was black and then she related that she had picked her colors quickly in her head. A moment had passed and then I had said that her loved ones would say *Hi* to her using the colors she had just picked. Another moment passed and the waiter put the salad she had ordered in front of her. On top of her salad was a big round black olive.

I looked at her and we were all smiling sooooo big. At that point I told her that the other color she had chosen was purple.

"You're right! How did you know that?" she asked.

"Your ring," I said. "I noticed it while you were eating and I know to pay attention to the little things. I asked the Unseen and was told that in fact, the purple in the ring you are wearing was one of the colors you had selected. You didn't say what colors you chose and so I didn't think I should say anything out loud unless you did."

Sarah then explained that the ring was from Scott, her boyfriend.

"Well, of course it is," I said.

We were standing up by this time, leaving the table, and Sarah looks at Debbie and asked what color Debbie had chosen. Debbie had a grandmother she was very close to and still felt very close to who was "dead." Both Sarah and I knew that Debbie had picked a color as well when I had told Sarah to choose one, but I had said at the time that they didn't have to tell me what colors they had chosen. I wasn't the one that needed to know.

Debbie said, "Oh, I picked a silly color. Don't even know why I picked it."

I looked at her and said, "Deb, you picked pink." Her eyes went wide and I said again, "It was pink you picked, wasn't it?"

Then it was Debbie's turn to look at me a mazed. "How did you know that?" she asked. I was about to say that it was my job to know, when I realized that is not what this is about. I am not here to play middleman for anybody. I am here to help show everyone we *don't need a middleman.* WE ARE ALL SPOKEN TO—IN ALL WAYS—ALWAYS. It is "just" a matter of knowing that.

I explained to Debbie that over a number of months, several friends and acquaintances of mine had lost grandmas, moms, and old female friends. Almost all of these women who had "crossed over" had said *Hi* to me using pink. It was over this same period of time I had finally read Dr. Doreen Virtue's *Divine Guidance*[1], which was an excellent and wondrous book that had helped me tremendously in achieving a better, clearer "connection" with the Unseen around me. The cover of her book is in pink and black. I had come to understand that to me, anyway, pink was being shown to represent Ancient Female Wisdom. I knew Debbie was thinking of her grandma when she was choosing colors and I had an "intuition" that she had picked pink.

I am saying all this to Debbie and Sarah as we are walking out of the restaurant. As we come out to the street, a woman comes walking by us wearing a bright pink sweater. We all started laughing and several "Oh, my Gods!" were uttered. We ended up following her because she was walking in the same direction as we were headed to our cars. I continued to explain that I have come to believe that we are ALL connected in some physical way that we just can't see. I believe we are all *literally* connected with what I call the "silver threads of Life's energy." I picture these threads as incredibly finer than the thread a spider uses to weave a web. Have you ever noticed one strand of a spider's thread blowing in a breeze? Depending on how the light is hitting it, the thread seems to be visible and then becomes invisible . . . whether you see it or not, it is there; can't change what Is.

This woman wearing pink had been walking in front of us all this time and she gets to her car before we do. She climbs in behind the wheel of her silver Mercedes.

***

Were Debbie, Sarah, and I being "spoken" to? Communicated with? Was Rebecca sent Love from her father via a painted ribbon of yellow? That is the decision you must make. I know my Truth in those moments. You must choose your own.

Please know that if you think that what has been written here is nothing more than a bunch of non sense, that is perfectly okay!!!—with me and with God. If you do not believe that there even is a God, that is just fine. We are all on our own path, living our own Way and this is, was, and always will be as it is supposed to be—it Is what it Is...perfect.

I have written this book for those who are beginning to understand and know as I know that the time of us thinking we need a middleman (or woman) to speak to God is coming to an end. The Time of accepting the *Know Ledge* that we are all Communicated with by God everyday, that we are "spoken to" through our thoughts by the Unseen around us is at hand...ours to grasp...to know, to hold...that also Is what it Is. The "random" music and dialogue, noises that surround us, are used to send us this knowledge. This Holy Dialogue – this *Godsign* - is in our words, our numbers, our colors, our sounds, our sights...all coincidences, all events that coincide are profound—pro found—a positive find. The coincidences that happen in your life are Speaking to you of direction; they are Gifts arranged for, and then sent to you by God.

This knowledge, this Knowing, this Way of living is the Garden...it is Eden. We have never truly left; we just told ourselves we had as we forgot that God surrounds us with His Love and Communicates that Message *to each of us daily.* When we as a species forgot that Truth, we walked out of our Garden of Eden. You need only to remember that you are all ways a Part of God to walk back in. You will come to know that God is everywhere and anywhere, at all times, in all ways. *Always.* It is only a matter of time before this truth is yours to accept, to know, and to live. It may not be this lifetime but during some lifetime of yours...this *know ledge* is yours to climb, claim, and KNOW. You can do it now, you can do it later...your choice.

At the time of this writing, it has been a few years since Gary's "death." To say that he and I have "come a long Way, baby" is an understatement. I now teach people to "read" the Godsign™ of their Uni Verse. A glorious dichotomy in life is that there is One Universe and there are billions of universes. I have my universe, you have yours, the lady down the street with all the cats and dogs has hers. We are all in this together in our One Universe and we each have our own perspective that creates our uniquely individual universe. The Unseen surrounding Us uses your own personal set of "symbols" in your daily life to say hello, to send you Love, and to let each of us know we are never alone! You no longer need to believe that you must have a middleman or woman to speak to God; God speaks to you everyday using Godsign™...you need only remember and believe that Truth.

We do many things backward in this physical reality and much of our backward thinking is in our words. We don't say that we are raised Up in love; we don't say that we are held in love...we say we have "fallen" in love. That is backward thinking. Another backward thought is that "seeing is believing." Is that what the Wright Brothers did? Did they *see* someone flying a plane and only then believe it was possible? We would not have come this far if the phrase "seeing is believing" were Truth. Rather, *it is in believing that we see!*

Will you believe for just a little while—"Just Believe"—in order to See? The color you chose and the number you just picked has set the alarm clock in your Universe. You may hit the snooze button; it is perfectly okay and a totally respectable thing to do. Digest the information you have just taken in with the reading of this book. Your alarm clock will go off again. Humanity (human unity), we as a people, a study in God's Love, are waking Up. A mom, dad, a husband, wife, grandparent, son, daughter or best buddy that you believe is "dead" and gone from you has worked from the Other Side to make sure this story ends up in your hands. Don't believe me? With the color you just picked, this loved One is going to communicate with you in the next few days. It may be in a candy wrapper at your feet, a group of flowers you pass by, the color that saturates an ad on your TV, or in the words of a song over the radio waves. Your entire world can be used to do this because They can use the entire world to send you Their Love.

There is a price to gain this Knowledge...a fee you must pay. You must "pay" attention. Watch for the little things in life when a "thought" of this loved One that you believe is "dead" comes into "your thoughts," look at what is around you, where you are, what is being said or shown to you, what sounds are in the background—what color or colors are near you, what "time" is being shown to you on whatever clock is near. We have gone digital with our clocks for a Reason. The numbers are being used to speak to us in all moments of time.

Your loved Ones on the Other Side—in the Unseen around you—your family and friends who Love you dearly hold your butterfly wings for you. They will help God help you through your metamorphosis. Your journey is unique, incredible, and a mazing and worth all the energy, time, thought, and Love you put into it. No two wing patterns on a butterfly are ever the same, and no two pilgrimages through a "meta" morphosis are alike. (Imagine us coming up with the word *meta*morphosis for what a caterpillar goes through to become a butterfly.) Your glory Us wings will be attached to you with the bindings from tears of pure joy that are created by you during your Sacred Journey.

But in the beginning this is *your* choice...always.

For that is the Way of Love.

Is Love that big? What do you think?

I live on the know ledge that Love Is....

Always...in All Ways.

Alarm Clock to a Butterfly

An alarm clock went off in my universe
and there is no way to prepare,
when the Unseen becomes visible
and what was hidden, suddenly clear.

The snooze button I promptly hit
as any fuzzy slug would do.
Just an overactive imagination,
turning one reality into two.

But a mazing coincidences multiplied
like an abacus of karmic events.
A bouquet of yellow splendor
finally woke me to life's Relevance.

Truth was revealed in stages,
like stairs leading up to a door,
knowing as I crossed each threshold
a dissolved mystery would lead to one more.

The Music Man began his Symphony
surrounding my world with the lyrical.
Rhapsodic communion of Truth and Love
composing my Opus of Miracles.

Waves of sound flowed daily
harmoniously echoing my thoughts.
Questions answered, solutions revealed
until for my sanity I fought.

When what you live sounds crazy,
how does one speak out loud?
The impossibilities I experienced
would seem absurd to most of the crowd.

Conversations with Walsh shown forth
to Highlight the path of my trip.
Yes, our Creator was conversing with me;
in deed designing this metamorphosis.

A binding of ribbons was sent,
actually some were there in plain sight.
The messages swept through in color;
consciously, unconsciously, day, night.

My Sculptor knew of perfection
choosing which shades to use and when,
'til I was wrapped in a shimmering rainbow,
comforted and cocooned within.

As a butterfly I emerged
and went soaring into the sky.
In Love my Creator whispered,
"Always remember with Whom you do fly."

A butterfly in the Garden, © Annie

Acknowledgements

There are so many I need to thank for their love, guidance, help and inspiration while living the journey that was to become *A butterfly in the Garden*. The first one I need to thank is The First One, our Creator; the One, Omnipotent, Omnipresent, all inclusive Source. Dear God, it is You who creates our possibilities in the First Place in the hope that our sacred potential will be achieved and shared in Love with the many sacred variations of YOU in our world. Thanks with all my heart for sharing all of You.

I wish to thank my dear friend Gary and my son Jake, who along with my Spirit, helped wake Up my heart and my mind. When many in this world would say he was long gone and "dead" Gary was the first to show me in this life, literally, that we all go through the process we call death BUT *none of us ceases to exist in that moment*. Learning about and communicating with Jake proved it to me. We drop the "body" but we are still very much a life. They are both very much still alive . .. alive in Spirit. . . just depends on your definition of Life. That Life Force of energy can Speak to all of us in more Ways than can be described here.

I wish to thank my friends and family who were mad because they are pro life and thought this book was pro choice; and thank you to my family and friends who were mad because they are pro choice and thought this a pro life book. It was my deepest hope that this was written in a balanced way that supported neither belief and illustrated the fact that your life, my life, ***anyone's life - never ends***. It is my hope that we can start to look at this discussion from a third perspective It is not whether someone "chooses to take" a life but rather to understand that the Spirit – the essence of a person is never really gone. When you realize and know that

169

we never cease to exist and start to look at the problem from that perspective, new answers, new Ways come to each of us.

A big THANK YOU I LOVE YOU ALL to my family and friends; my husband, my children, my parents, my brothers, sisters, aunts, uncles, cousins (birth and in-law and everything else, we are all sisters and brothers in this world). Because your love is so much a part of my life, I was led to know that we all share the profound love, pleasure and experience of communicating with the *unseen* Spirit surrounding us. My gratitude and love for you is more than words here can truly express. Thank you very, very much!

My eternal gratitude to all the musicians, music men and music women who were in large part responsible for Waking me Up to all the possibilities in life. Your inspiration, the Blessings found in your Sound - your words, your music, your songs have changed so many lives on so many levels. You are all walking Angels wherever you are and I am forever grateful for the Gift of you!

To Martha Graves, who believed in me whole heartedly doing an AWESOME job of editing *A butterfly in the Garden*. Martha, you helped me know that God's Work is worth the effort and I am eternally grateful for your Light, your Walk, your Gifts and all the Healing you bring to our world! You ROCK sister friend. Thank you dearly.

Mere words are not enough to thank all those in Spirit - the Angels, Guides and muses, friends, family, loved ones. Thanks for speaking to me whenever, wherever, all the time, always, in all Ways. Thanks to John, Brigid, Johnny, Mary Ruth, Lucille, Nell, the Ellens, the Marks, the Bills, Will, the Evelyns, the Saras, the Pauls, Beckie, Joanie, Richard, Lou, Kim, Betty, Arni, Abbey, Greg, Ian, Scott, Thomas, Elvis, Art, Abe, Jack, Andrew, Francis, Patrick, Abraham, Buddha, Master Usui, Rumi, Dr. Maxwell, Yellow Feather, Joy and my friend Yeshua Ben Joseph, dearest Jesus. Thank YOU doesn't begin to cover the gratitude and Love I wish to express to you all for your support, guidance, Conversations and Godsigns. It is thanks to you that I remember now who I am. It is only a matter of Time before we are all in Spirit together again. Thank you for the enduring and never-ending Journey. May I be of help bringing your Light and Love into our world. I sincerely look forward to the *Sacred Dance* and being able to express mySelf in the Holy Way to my God and you All, when together again in Spirit.

With my deep gratitude and love always,

- *Annie oxooxo*

Contact Information:

Godsign Institute
www.godsigninstitute.com
info@godsigninstitute.com

Progressive Spiritualist Church
www.progressivespiritualist.org

NOTES

Chapter II

1. *Cruisin'*
   © William "Smokey" Robinson and Marvin Tarplin,
   Crusin', performed by Smokey Robinson and
   The Miracles on *The Ballad Album*, Motown
   Legends, 1995.

2. *Iris*
   Goo Goo Dolls.
   John Rzeznik, EMI Virgin Songs, Inc./Scrap
   Metal Music.
   Produced by Rob Cavallo and Goo Goo Dolls
   Warner Bros. Records. BMI Administered by EMI
   Virgin Music, Inc.

3. **City of Angels**–Soundtrack
   Produced by Danny Bramson
   © 1998 Warner Bros. Records, Inc.
   Album Executive Producers: Charles Roven,
   Scott Welch, Pat Magnarella and Brad Silberling

4. *Your Song*
   Written by Elton John and Bernie Taupin
   Produced by Gus Dudgeon   ©1969 Dick James
   Music, Ltd. Administered by Songs of PolyGram
   International, Inc.

5. *You Make Loving Fun*
   Written by Christine McVie
   ©1976 by Gentoo Music, Inc.

6. ***Can You Feel The Love Tonight***
Written by Elton John and Tim Rice
©1994 Wonderland Music Company, Inc.
Produced by Chris Thomas

Chapter IV

1. The Rider-Waite Tarot Deck®
Is a registered trademark of
U.S. Games Systems, Inc.
Also known as the Waite® Tarot
Conceived by Arthur Edward Waite
Card design by Pamela Coleman Smith™.

2. ***Can't Help Falling In Love***
Written by George Weiss, Hugo Peretti and Luigi
Creatore, is a pop song based on "Plaisir d'amour" by
Jean Paul Egide Martini. It was rewritten for the 1961
film *Blue Hawaii*, starring Elvis Presley.

Chapter VII

1. ***That's The Way It Is***
Written by M. Martin, K. Lundin, A. Carlsson
Produced by Max Martin and Kristina Lundin for
Cheiron Productions.   ©1999 Sony Music
Entertainment

2. ***My Heart Will Go On*** - (Love Theme from Titanic)
Written by James Horner, Will Hennings
Famous Music Corp. on behalf of TCG Music
Publishing, Inc. Produced and Arranged by Walter
Afanasieff - Co-produced by James Horner.

3. ***My Heart Will Go On*** - (Love Theme from Titanic)
   Written by James Horner, Will Hennings
   Famous Music Corp. on behalf of TCG Music
   Publishing, Inc. Produced and Arranged by Walter
   Afanasieff Co-produced by James Horner.

4. ***That's The Way It Is***
   Written by M. Martin, K. Lundin, A. Carlsson
   Produced by Max Martin and Kristina Lundin for
   Cheiron Productions. ©1999 Sony Music
   Entertainment

5. ***Faithfully***
   Written by J. Cain
   From the Journey album FRONTIERS
   Produced by Mike Stone for Mike Stone
   Enterprises, Ltd. and Ken Elson for Elson Music
   Vision. ©1983 Weed High Nightmare Music

6. ***Yellow***
   Written by Coldplay: Chris Martin, Guy Berryman,
   Jon Buckland and Will Champion ©2000 Coldplay

7. ***Conversations with God: an uncommon dialogue,
   Book 1***
   Page 58 ©Neale Donald Walsch.
   All rights reserved. G.P. Putnam's Sons – member of
   Penguin Putnam, Inc. Used by permission.

8. ***Conversations with God: an uncommon dialogue,
   Book 1***
   Page 20 © Neale Donald Walsch.
   All rights reserved. G.P. Putnam's Sons – member of
   Penguin Putman, Inc. Used by permission.

Chapter VIII

1. ***Conversations with God: an uncommon dialogue,
   Book 3***
   Pages 246 – 250   ©Neale Donald Walsch.
   All rights reserved. Hampton Roads Publishers.
   Used by permission.

Chapter IX

1. ***Conversations with God: an uncommon dialogue,
   Book 3***
   Page 63   ©Neale Donald Walsch.
   All rights reserved. Hampton Roads Publishers.
   Used by permission.

2. ***Rock This Town***
   © Brian Setzer A song written by Brian Setzer and
   performed by the **Stray Cats** from their UK debut
   album *Stray Cats*. Its first US Release was on the
   1982 album *Built for Speed*.

Made in the USA
Charleston, SC
18 October 2011